AND McKELLAR

DESTINED TO HEAL

BIOGRAPHY OF AN AMAZING SPIRITUAL
HEALER

BY
ROS JONES

G V JONES
HAMPSHIRE

Design: Ros Jones and Judith Blake
Printed by: Sarsen Press, Winchester, Hampshire, UK
First published by: Gethyn Jones, Hampshire, UK   2003

www.andrewmckellar.com

ISBN 0-9545068-0-4

*For further information about Andrew McKellar and his healing work please log on to his website: **www.andrewmckellar.com***

CONTENTS

Chapter		Page
Foreword – "2001"		i
1	"2003"	3
2	**Childhood – Andrew's Words**	13
	Patient Testimonies – "Cancer"	25
3	**Bad Health, Bedsits and Breaking Point**	31
	Patient Testimonies – "Bones"	41
4	**Beginning to Heal and Sai Baba**	49
	Patient Testimonies – "Accidental Injuries"	64
5	**"Helpers"**	67
	Patient Testimonies – "Other Conditions"	76
6	**New Horizons**	85
7	**Endings, Beginnings and Dreams**	99
	"Marcus"	107
8	**Good Press, Bad News**	109
	"Bluey"	118
9	**Bag of Tools and Colour Chart**	121
	"Wallpaper"	133
10	**Separate Paths, Moving Words**	137

DEDICATION

I would like to take this opportunity to send my heartfelt thanks and gratitude to this biography's author, Ros Jones – for the dedication and love she has channelled through her writing. Many have tried before, but the book - or books - never came to fruition. Now I know why Ros was chosen to write this book. Thanks Ros – I will always be forever grateful.

Also, thanks to broadcaster and producer Gethyn Jones. Firstly, for his awareness in realising the importance of my work and, secondly, for the dedication and love that he too has shown in making an increasing number of people aware of the vast power that flows from my hands. It is very difficult to find a true friend these days. In Gethyn and Ros Jones – and I speak hand on heart – I have true friends and I pray to the powers that be that our friendship may travel far, even beyond this earthly existence.

Maggie and Lucy deserve thanks too for their dedicated support. I will always be there if they need me. And to my friend Mick Ingram I must say: thanks for being there.

I would also like to thank my wife Gerri for all her support. I know we have both learnt so much over the past seven years. We have experienced five home moves, much toil and trouble, considerable pain and grief. Wow, have we been put to the test. With your power of mediumship, Gerri, you have helped enormously. That's some praise, given that you know what I think by and large of mediums and healers alike – ie keep well away from most of them because there is only a small handful of natural born mediums and healers, destined to work for Spirit. Quite frankly, forget the rest. Always consult the best. Anything less will just be weak power.

Gerri, your mediumship and pure proof of life after death have helped so many. You shun publicity. You do your work in such a quiet way. I have experienced your abilities first hand and, like so many others, must thank you for being there over the years. I am sorry that I put our relationship under pressure with the inevitable publicity and fame that comes with successful healing. There you were, never even wanting to make ripples while I was busy creating tidal waves. I thank you again. May the Great Buddha guide you and keep you safe. I will never forget you.

Lastly, my thanks to the late Ted Fricker, an incredible healer - never properly appreciated whilst alive. It was Ted who provided the title for this biography – still an inspiration from "beyond". Still working.

Much love,

Andy

For Ted Fricker

In admiration of his excellent work.

Then and now.

FOREWORD

FOREWORD

"2001"

"Faith is not belief without proof, but trust without reservation"

I first contacted Andrew McKellar on Monday 30th April 2001. I had telephoned him, in the full knowledge that all I would get was his answerphone. He didn't disappoint. Somewhat sheepishly, I left a short message. And prepared to wait. For as long as it took.

It had only been the previous Friday that a friend had provided me, out of the blue, with Andrew's personal telephone number. Admittedly, the "friend", Stephen Smith, is a young psychic medium and spiritual healer in the South of England and I had just spent an hour with him, during which time he had hit upon the only topic I hoped he wouldn't: my beautiful, talented, witty and adorable sister Hazel had cancer. So there it was – out of his mouth, with no prompting from mine. And there we sat, silently, while Stephen searched for the words to offer some hope. But Stephen, by his own admission, had had no success to date with the dreaded condition.

He did, however, know a man that had.

Hazel had been diagnosed with cancer of the lung in the autumn of 1999. Her cancer consultant had outlined her options to her, an operation not being one of them. Fast-forward to Christmas and she was the other side of radiotherapy – tired, burned, off her food – but here at least. By June 2000 her tumour was undetectable and life returned to as normal as it was going to get. But by April 2001 "it" was back and options were once again reviewed, including the non-option of an operation. And so she progressed to … Hello! Chemotherapy time, which she would also come through – tired, off her food, bald and back at home in Wiltshire.

Cue answerphone message to Andrew McKellar. And that's when it all began. He rang me back. The same morning. He had a cancellation for the following afternoon – 1.20 pm, Tuesday 1st May. I took it.

My next problem, ironically, was Hazel. I hadn't actually *told* her that I was telephoning a spiritual healer, who'd had more than a bit of a result treating cancer. I'd imagined months of waiting to receive a return call from Mr McKellar. And here I was, custodian of a precious appointment

i

with the man himself – tomorrow – in Southampton, when she lived near Bath … I rang her.

Hazel had, understandably, given up on a "normal" routine, preferring to stay in bed that much longer each day, reading, sleeping, "hiding under the covers", as she put it. Away from food and the once-welcome odours wafting through the house from the kitchen cooking. Not hiding from the awful, non-negotiable, eternally present fact that she had cancer. Just coping in her own personal way. Just getting through.

And suddenly, here I was on the telephone to her, gaily suggesting that she might like to travel the next morning to Burridge, Southampton to meet a spiritual healer. Gently prodding her just to "consider" the possibility, when a trip to her bathroom was a mile and a half in itself and a journey in a car Mount Everest. So she said yes. Because that was Hazel. The "deal" was that I would get up early, shoot to her home in Box (two hours), drive her to Andrew McKellar (one and a half hours), drive back to Box (ditto) and return home to Gosport on the South Coast all in the same day (another two hours).

And we did just that. I arrived far too early at her home (desperate not to be late for Andrew) to be greeted by the sound of reluctant movement upstairs. Hazel was "up", descending the stairs, bemoaning the fact that she would need a sandwich for the car, resenting the fact that food had to be discussed, but the cocktail of drugs she needed to see her through each day demanded her enemy – food. And so it went on until she was installing herself in my passenger seat and we were Burridge-bound.

Burridge. Not a village name that screams famous out of the atlas. So it's just as well that I believe that coincidences are anything but. I had only recently relocated back down South from London. I had found a job in Southampton and, preferring to avoid the motorway to-ing and fro-ing to work, I had plotted a route on the A-road. And, wouldn't you know it, when I needed to find Andrew McKellar's healing sanctuary in rural Burridge (he had literally just moved there in the Spring of 2001), there it was, effortlessly positioned on my daily route. We arrived an hour early.

As is the way of human nature, we sat in Andrew's road, second-guessing what we were going to find. Just what had we let ourselves in for? Would it all be a con? Was my shuttle-service a waste of time and energy? Were we being fleeced? The list was limitless. Our cynicism had suddenly gone orbital. But time was ticking and there was nothing for it. Into the breach. And, looking back, I realise that this was probably all part of it – Andrew's healing touch. It had begun. I had collected a weary, bruised and slow motion sister and, suddenly, here she was sitting next to me in a steamed-up car grinning from ear to ear with a "what-am-I-like?" expression. My Hazel was back in business.

What happened next was like clockwork. The house was lovely. There were no embarrassing introductions on the doorstep. You let yourself in; you took a seat in a bright and welcoming waiting room. You quickly drank in the various "spiritual" references – the Sai Baba bust, various Red Indian statues and an impressive selection of articles to browse through, both on the wall and to take away. And, just to overcome any embarrassing silence whilst waiting to be seen, there was a TV in the corner with a video playing on a loop with seemingly endless interviews between Andrew McKellar and his patients, each one the same:

"Andrew cured me."

Enter Andrew. *"Hazel, hi – come through."* As simple as that. All that remained of my sister were her shoes until, smiling and calm she re-emerged, healing session number one done and dusted and a new appointment for the following Monday firmly in her diary. The Monday was a UK Bank Holiday. It hadn't even occurred to Andrew McKellar. Presumably, it was just another working day. I, of course, was full of questions. What had it been like? - What do you mean, you saw colours? - Really? Were his hands really that hot? We took ourselves to a little café in the next village and sat with tea and cheese scones just to wind down in anticipation of the miles back to Wiltshire. And Hazel tucked in, smiling and chatty. Almost like there was absolutely nothing wrong. Did she believe that he had 'something'? As I recall, she said she'd like to think so.

We actually managed another two healing appointments with Andrew until, quite suddenly, Hazel was offered that elusive operation by a cancer specialist in another West Country hospital. Surgical techniques had moved on just in the short space of time that my sister had known about her tumour. And so June 2001 saw her operation go ahead, a post-operative view from her surgeon that he had been able to remove all of the tumour and then months of recuperation in Wiltshire.

Interestingly enough, her surgeon had found that the tumour was practically "dead". Hazel confided in a telephone call to me that she wanted very much to believe that Andrew McKellar had played his part in such a result. *"Who knows?"*, she said. *"Makes you wonder, doesn't it?"* And really knowing seemed irrelevant anyway. It was simply good news and in her shoes that was miracle enough.

Now, however, the trips to Andrew were simply out of the question. She just had to focus on building up her strength. And who would blame her. If she couldn't travel to see Andrew, then someone else would be able to and they would receive the same "lift" that such a visit can afford.

Spring 2002 came and Hazel was on the ski slopes. But it wasn't to be. The tumour returned and August Bank Holiday saw her back in the operating theatre in Bristol, followed by precious days at the wonderful Dorothy House Hospice in Bradford-on-Avon. On October 20th 2002 Hazel died.

Looking back, one inevitably tries to relive conversations and efforts made to help. Often, in times when she was feeling reasonably fit, Hazel would say *"I really ought to see Andrew again you know."* But life presents a variety of demands and ups and downs – a husband, two children at school, her Samaritans' work, the supermarket, social commitments, holidays even…

And, actually, whether or not one believes that a truly gifted spiritual healer can actually "cure" a life-threatening or terminal medical condition, is perhaps not what it's all about. Often, at a time when all hope has been removed by medical experts, what a person requires is a different focus and a return to "normality". An opportunity to take responsibility not just for their physical health but for their mental well being too. What a person can discover with the help of an Andrew is a wealth of surprises: a release of stress, tension and anxiety; a remarkable end to discomfort and pain; opportunities to throw away painkilling drugs - in themselves anguish-laden to a patient, as quantities required to ease pain get higher and higher; a surge in energy levels enabling them to feel back in control of their destiny; life-threatening symptoms just disappearing; tumours dispersing altogether. The list is endless, mind-boggling and certainly not just about cancer.

Andrew McKellar has devoted his life to working with the sick. Andrew McKellar gave my sister an appointment on 30th April 2001. And he gave her hope.

Andrew McKellar works with spirit doctors to transform his patients' lives. Andrew McKellar talks to dead people. He is on a mission to heal. He asks for a donation that wouldn't fund a round of drinks in a pub. He believes he has a rare and god-given gift. Day after day he places his hands on people, who arrive with terrible problems and leave with heart-warming experiences and smiles. For those who question endlessly how anyone can believe that miracles can happen, perhaps they might ask themselves why should he bother? Why open himself up to ridicule, disdain, scepticism and downright abuse? If those disbelievers could just suspend their misgivings for a moment .... Now, that would be progress.

It is an honour and a pleasure to write this book and long overdue.

Ros Jones

What is dying?

I am standing upon that foreshore.
A ship at my side spreads her white sails
to the morning breeze
and starts for the blue ocean.

She is an object of beauty and strength
and I stand and watch her until, at length,
she hangs like a speck of white clouds
just where the sea and sky come down
to mingle with each other.

Then someone at my side says,
"There! She's gone!"

"Gone where?"

"Gone from my sight, that's all."

She is just as large in mast and spar and hull
as ever she was when she left my side;
just as able to bear her load of living freight
to the place of her destination.
Her diminished size *is in me*, not in her.

And just at that moment
when someone at my side says
"There! She's gone!",
there are other eyes watching
her coming
and other voices ready
to take up the glad shout
"Here she comes!"

And that is dying.

Victor Hugo

CHAPTER ONE

CHAPTER ONE

"2003"

"The more you judge, the less you love"

February 12th 2003, a wet and chilly Wednesday evening and I am sitting with spiritual healer Andrew McKellar in the reassuringly warm family sitting room of his present house in Southampton. This is the private part of the home he shares with his wife Gerri, children Kristie-Anne and Marcus and an assortment of highly entertaining, people-friendly animals.

Across the hall is his Healing Sanctuary - the equally welcoming space he has carefully set aside for his patients. They attend for healing each week, eager to place their trust in a man who, in turn, places his hands on them to do whatever he can to help. Some arrive sceptically, some are returning for treatment sessions, having experienced the effectiveness of his healing previously. And some arrive believing already. It really doesn't matter to Andrew McKellar. They come anyway. In the course of their healing sessions, he will bring them hope, relief from pain, lessening of terrifying and difficult symptoms and, often, a complete cure from their illness.

As far as Andrew is concerned, there is absolutely no ailment his healing powers can't tackle. From migraines to arthritis, Crohn's Disease to rheumatism, bothersome cysts to tumours with the worst possible prognoses. "Can't" is simply not in the McKellar vocabulary. He's "zapped" his own serious health problems in the past, so he should know.

So, a miracle worker? Andrew McKellar will look you straight in the eye and confirm emphatically yes. How he came to be in this position is finally about to go down on record. It is no mean task, which accounts for what he teasingly refers to as my "house brick" – a chunky, past its sell-by date lump of a cassette recorder, strategically placed between the two of us on the table to enable me to capture all his words. Truth be told, it could benefit itself from the regenerative powers of Andrew's hands but I refrain from cracking a cheap joke. We are meeting to tell Andrew's story so far.

Andrew and Gerri

Andrew with step-daughter Kristie-Anne

This will be a journal of his life "to date". And, as I quickly realise, it will contain far more heartache, suffering and sorrow than one could ever suspect just by meeting him in his lovely home. So, this will be a vital time – an opportunity for Andrew to reveal just how an individual can overcome enormous hardship, illness and persistent disappointments to follow a pathway to success.

"Sai" – one half of a double act!

"Baba" Andrew's shadow

Andrew now has a dream – or, rather a dream "portfolio". He plans this book of his life; then there will be the website; in turn, he will be creating and recording spiritually inspired healing CDs and commissioning an illuminating and uplifting video. What's more, the website will allow him to welcome numbers of needy patients on a scale he simply couldn't entertain were he to remain just Andrew McKellar, home-based healing sanctuary. He will soon be able to provide Absent Healing services to anyone in need, wherever their home. Failure is not an option. Why should it be? Andrew was told when he was in his teens that he was one of the "chosen few":

"Andrew – one day you are going to be performing a special task and you will be segregated from the normal routine of life."

Career advice? No. This was a message he received loud and clear on more than one occasion as a young man. From people in the know. From people he trusted. From dead people.

Suddenly, Andrew is transporting me back to his earliest memories and it quickly becomes apparent that I shall have my work cut out keeping pace with the geography of his early moves. For by the age of six Andrew McKellar was fast negotiating what sounds like Southampton's very own Monopoly Board. Born on 21st November 1962 in the City's Chapel Road docks area, his family had moved not long afterwards to Lime Street; swiftly followed by Vine Road; finally dropping anchor in the Shirley Warren suburb, allowing Andrew to see through, somewhat reluctantly, his education at a selection of Shirley Warren state schools.

Times were rarely easy for the family. It was a "making ends meet" sort of existence. No "Advance to Go and collect £200" in the process. The McKellar "Chance" cards were always more likely to demand moving back three spaces on the board.

He has two younger brothers – Michael and Kenny - now both in their thirties. Their father, Malcolm, was a chef in the Merchant Navy, which predictably meant absences from home. A dour Scot, he had inevitably been known as "Jock" for as long as Andrew can remember. Their mother, Maureen, worked as a Catering Assistant at Southampton Docks. Talking with Andrew McKellar about his early life, he happily tells it as it was and, on the face of it, one might be forgiven for assuming that his was a rather ordinary, unprivileged and routine sort of start in life.

Until you ask an innocent question, just by way of getting the full picture on the McKellar Family as it must have been for the young Andrew in the 1960s.

And your grandparents?

There is a silence while Andrew sorts out how to phrase his reply.

"Ah, well, I didn't ever know my grandparents on my father's side of the family. In point of fact, the man whom I saw as my father all my life wasn't actually my real dad."

What had in fact happened was that Andrew's mother had met his real father in 1961. She had become pregnant with Andrew and, on finding out, Andrew's real father had, in Andrew's words, *"done a bunny hop, never to be seen again."*

There is no sign of resentment or judgement. As I will come to expect from our chats together, Andrew McKellar simply tells it as it is. And, the fact is that suddenly I am altering the details on his early family life, for now his two younger brothers become half-brothers, he has a non-blood relative in his father and one begins to wonder what sort of effect such details may have had on his childhood happiness.

It seems logical to ask about his maternal grandparents. Yes, indeed, he had known them, *"although we didn't have much to do with them."* He wasn't exaggerating. It transpires that the children saw them *"probably half a dozen times"* when they were growing up. Making such a statement seems as easy as reading out a shopping list to Andrew. This was obviously the norm for Andrew and his siblings.

We discuss what type of friends he had. His hobbies and interests. Judging by his reply, they were a normal crowd of lads and an equally normal selection of pastimes. He liked cycling and swimming – mostly with his friends; he enjoyed playing harmonica and, in time, would teach himself the guitar; as a teenager he adopted the full teddy boy uniform – the quiff, the bootlace, the drape, the winklepickers and a crowd of lookalikes to hang out with. Andrew grins delightedly at the memory. He indulged his passion for Fifties and Sixties rock and roll music and intimates that he ran into trouble on more than one occasion in these early formative years. Because teddy boys did.

And then we rewind to talk about Andrew's very first years in the McKellar family and, just as normally as he has talked about the family's homes and their liking for cats as pets, he begins to talk about the people who used to visit him in bed at night.

And you know that this was no ordinary childhood.

Baby Andrew in the early 1960s

Andrew aged 10 with Michael and Kenny

Andrew in his teddy boy days

UNSEEN FRIENDS

There are eyes that watch over us
every single day

There are eyes that watch over us
while we are here to stay.

We are given guidance
in our lives, from unseen friends

They give us guidance in our lives
right to the very end.

If we link to power within
we can know our unseen friends

If we link to power within
more guidance shall we gain.

If we look back over many years
we can surely say

How did we make it
through difficult times

Was there guidance along the way?

2 February 1991
Andrew McKellar

CHAPTER TWO

CHAPTER TWO

CHILDHOOD
Andrew's Words

"Faith sees the invisible

Feels the intangible

And achieves the impossible"

"As a young child I was always aware when I was lying in bed in the evenings that there were people standing around the bed. I couldn't always see these people but I knew they were there."

This is a regular sort of statement that Andrew McKellar throws into the conversation as we look back on his formative years. After a while, one finds oneself going with the flow, as comfortable with talking about these visitors, voices and "felt" presences as one might be catching up on the latest TV soap gossip.

"There was a group of people – one particular gentleman – tall with an eye-patch – there most evenings until I was about thirteen, I think. He looked Victorian; fatherly, in his 40ies. There were others with him – a mix of grown-ups. They'd stay five minutes or so."

I am itching to ask Andrew whether or not he used to ask them questions. Like what were they doing there? It also occurs to me that he probably shared a bedroom, at least with one brother. Didn't they ever notice anything strange?

Andrew always gives the fullest reply that he can, which is just as well because it is a lot for one to take in if one's own childhood memories don't run to resident "higher beings".

"I used to say 'Hello' or 'Welcome' but actually that particular group of visitors never spoke. No one in my family had psychic interests. As far

back as I can remember (probably about age two and a half) anything featuring psychic phenomena held an attraction for me. Yes, I shared a room with Kenny but he seemed unaware of anything."

"I would look in the bedroom wardrobe mirror at a glow around my body. Friends couldn't see it. I was surprised one day when I mentioned it to my father. He asked how long I'd been seeing it and I said for as long as I could remember. He said it was strange because he had been sitting on the boat deck one day in the Merchant Navy and a deck hand had said 'Jock – I can see all these colours around your body – what's going on?' It was probably the only time apart from when he was ill later in his life that he actually showed any interest."

Apart from his silent visitors, Andrew's out of the ordinary experiences grew as he did. From the age of five he vividly remembers regular "out of the body" experiences prompting him to ask: *Who am I? What am I doing in my body?*

"I would be hovering over trees and housetops – up through the ceiling and off. As soon as I left my body there was light in the room, even though it was dark. I used to see lights – trails of light – shooting across the room. I still see them, even when it's light. Bursts of blue light. The people were always there with me – even when we moved house."

It seems appropriate at this stage to prod a little bit deeper into the McKellar family's reaction to their eldest son's daily life. Andrew had clearly got the impression at a very tiny age that presenting them with a run-down of his spiritual social diary didn't generate a positive response but he persevered because he didn't doubt his reality.

"I would have very vivid dreams, including premonitions. They would always come true. I left it a few years before the experiences began to intensify and then I approached my Mum and Dad about it. Their reaction was that they didn't want to hear this nonsense. My father told my mother to take me to a psychiatrist. So I didn't say so much after that. Back in those days it was children should be seen and not heard."

When Andrew was eight or nine years of age he began to realise that he was seriously, unquestionably and undeniably different from other children. By now, he was naturally asking questions and not just prepared to sit back and accept that his seemingly unique experiences weren't actually fact. As children do, he would talk out loud to his parents, presumably assuming that they would have the answers.

"My Dad was always watching the horse racing or the boxing on TV and I would say to him 'I'm going to be on the television one day' and he would look at me and say 'Yeh, OK Andrew'. Or he would be reading the newspaper and I'd say 'Dad - I'll be in the newspaper one day'. He thought I was mad. Exaggerating. I said to both my parents – 'When I'm older I'm going to be extremely famous but I don't know what it is'. Nobody was interested in hearing about my experiences. I even tried with a couple of teachers at school and they said 'It's all in the mind. Don't be stupid'. I think to this very day the main mass of people in society are ignorant of who they are, what they are and what their capabilities are."

Andrew tells a charming and irresistibly cute story of another experience, which has remained with him since the age of ten. He went with his school on a camping trip. Andrew recalls how he wasn't in the least bit sport-inclined at that age and he also struggled to get on with the PE teacher, who was in charge of the children on the trip.

"I didn't get on with my PE teacher, Mr Cooper. At the time I wasn't sporty and would even forget my PE kit on purpose! Hard to believe now. I lift weights every day! Anyway, we pitched tent in a field in the New Forest near the farmhouse of Mr Cooper's parents. Mr Cooper was very strict and he said to us we could go to see the cow, Twisty, but we absolutely mustn't go near her calf, Toffee."

Toffee, it seems, had been born with a serious attitude problem. This was a bovine youngster with unnerving behavioural difficulties and the iron will of a Greta Garbo wanting to be alone. With hindsight and, not overlooking the obvious pun mileage, Mr Cooper's instructions were probably like a red rag to a bull for Andrew McKellar, aged ten. No sooner had Saturday morning arrived, Andrew had spotted Toffee the calf in the field. And he hadn't hesitated:

"*I lifted the gate, walked across the field and up to the calf. With that, Toffee just lay down, rolled over and allowed me to stoke her and put my arms around her. My teacher was running towards the field shouting 'Stay there! Stay there!'. I thought I was in big trouble but his parents wanted to come out and see what I'd done. They wanted to photograph what was happening because they just couldn't believe it.*"

So, was Andrew later chastised by the strict Mr Cooper? Not a bit of it. "*He invited me on the next trip free.*"

And Andrew would have loved to go, if only his father had permitted it. But, he wasn't allowed to go the next time and Andrew had to content himself with the knowledge that this was probably an early indication of the special and almost magical gift he held in his hands.

CHALLENGING ENCOUNTERS

Andrew, as the years progressed, came to accept that he seemed destined to confront puzzling experiences. He became more philosophical and accepting of the fact that family and friends simply wouldn't see or hear things first-hand, in the way that he did. Now a seasoned teenager and much more his own man, he *knew* that whatever he witnessed wasn't just down to a vivid imagination. The spiritual encounters weren't going to go away. On the contrary, they were beginning to accelerate.

And someone was definitely looking out for him. He recalls riding his bicycle down a very steep hill on a normally busy main road one day. He was coming up to an unavoidable right-hand turn but it wasn't a problem because, when he checked behind, there was fortuitously no one there:

"*I duly pulled out to turn right. But a very forceful and loud voice ordered 'Don't pull out Andrew and don't turn right'.*"

Luckily Andrew kept left. Had he not, a car that appeared from nowhere, speeding horrendously fast, would have ploughed into him.

Fourteen seems to have been a pivotal time for him. A year earlier his maternal grandmother had died. He remembers her as a sweet old lady, their "Nan", whom they barely ever saw when he was growing up. On her death, his uncle Brian (brother to Andrew's mother) took on Nan's house. Andrew recalls how at age fourteen he was asked to babysit there for uncle Brian and his wife Tina. They had two young babies. Andrew describes how he was alone in the house and standing in the upstairs bathroom. Both children were very little and, Andrew stresses, certainly not big enough to reach the level of a door handle. So when Andrew heard the bathroom door clearly open behind him he was somewhat startled:

"As I turned around, I saw the handle in the 'down' position and the door still opening. It then began to close and I reached across before the handle could retract, grabbed the door and held it open. But there was absolutely no one there. My uncle's collie dog Susie was looking up from the bottom of the stairs, whimpering and with all her hackles up. The children definitely weren't able to interfere with the door."

Shaken, Andrew sat downstairs on the settee, the dog still obviously distressed and firmly glued to his lap, awaiting uncle Brian's return. The experience, he hastens to add, wasn't frightening to him, more startling – *"the way you'd feel when something unexpected occurs. You immediately assume it could be a burglar."*

As soon as his uncle returned, Andrew told him what had happened. But, yet again, the response he received was frustratingly negative. Uncle Brian's main concern was that Andrew shouldn't mention anything to Tina. Andrew was forced to comply but by now was convinced that he had sensed his grandmother's presence.

It wouldn't be long before his intuition was proved correct. A few months later he was back at his uncle's house and, literally, on his way out of the front door, waving goodbye. And then he saw her, slowly walking past him and back into the house. No more than three feet from him and as solid and natural as the relatives he was bidding farewell. His grandmother - Nan - heading purposefully up the hallway and into her kitchen.

"My first reaction was simply to follow her. It seemed the natural thing to do. The lights were off in the kitchen, so I flicked them on but there was nothing there. This time I told my Mum what had happened. With hindsight, I think my mother was actually very intuitive and did believe in life after death. However, in those days she pooh-poohed it of course."

Yet again, a profound experience, which Andrew wanted to share with his close family, was in danger of being consigned to the "didn't happen" closet. His mother's response was a terse *"Andrew - let my Mum rest in peace."* His father's input was as brilliantly constructive as ever: *"There's something wrong with that nipper …"*

This time, however, Andrew was going to have his moment. Just a few weeks later when his father was away at sea, Andrew was awoken at around one o'clock in the morning, not by a spirit visitor but by his mother. Standing in his doorway, white faced and with her mouth opening and closing silently as she tried to speak, his mother was repeatedly pointing towards her own bedroom. Finally, after Andrew had asked her several times what on earth the matter was, she managed to get the words out: *"Mum's here."* She had woken up suddenly in bed, turned over and been confronted by her mother standing large as life against her bedroom wardrobe door. Andrew's mother may not have wanted to talk about it but at least she would now have no hiding place. Now she would be in a position to understand just how Andrew had been feeling during all those difficult years. It was a small step to help Andrew and his mother develop a closer relationship. But an important one. I make the point to Andrew as we discuss his grandmother's visits, that he runs the risk of seeing more of his Nan now that she's passed over than he ever did when he was growing up! He smiles at the irony.

And, even more ironically, uncle Brian may have thought that he could sweep Andrew's experiences under the carpet. But he too would soon be proved wrong. It seemed as if, finally, Andrew's spirit friends were making

Maureen McKellar – Andrew would grow very close to his mother later in life. Her photograph has pride of place in his Sanctuary

some sort of effort to prove to his doubting family that their "after physical death" presence was beyond derision or debate.

Sadly, tragedy was soon to strike uncle Brian's family. Brian and Tina's younger son, Tony, would die in an horrific accident. He was hit by a motorbike and, such was the impact of the accident to his head, he didn't stand a chance. Not long afterwards, Andrew recalls, the little boy came to him at home and spoke:

"Andy – I'm going to move the boxes in the loft. Also, tell Dad that the black dog was hit but it wasn't killed."

Andrew called his uncle to ask him over so that he could tell him privately what he'd heard. Brian was puzzled by both comments. However, he had to concede that the week before, Tina's brother had accidentally driven into a black labrador … and it had lived. True to form, nevertheless, Brian left Andrew's house in a sceptical frame of mind. This time, however, he would be telephoning Andrew soon afterwards to eat his words:

"Brian 'phoned me to say 'You're not going to believe what's happened. Our loft is locked. No one can get up there. We were lying in bed the other evening and we could hear movement in the loft. Tony's belongings had gone up there in boxes after he died, with masking tape to seal them. I went up to investigate and found the boxes all open and all the toys scattered over the floor. There were small footprints in the dust up there too'."

"I told him, as I had before, that there is no such thing as death. You cannot die."

And, maybe this time, Brian believed.

There is also a lovely postscript to this story. I ask Andrew if he ever goes to see psychic mediums. The withering look on his face speaks volumes. His response is a highly emphatic "no". He is at pains to tell me that he personally believes that the majority of "mediums" practising their spiritual craft are actually doing no such thing of the sort. They may not consciously know that they aren't producing genuine "evidence" of life after death, he believes. They're more often than not well-intentioned, good and kind folk. However, he is convinced that most are simply working on a physic "awareness" that absolutely everyone possesses. And for Andrew McKellar that's just not good enough.

He does, however, want to give full credit to Welsh medium Stephen O'Brien. He, Andrew enthuses, is "the business" – a phenomenal talent. And, when you hear Andrew's account of what happened one evening at a packed Southampton Guildhall evening of mediumship with Stephen O'Brien, you have to marvel at the accuracy of the information Andrew was given.

Andrew was sitting in the audience, mildly curious but not expecting to be addressed personally by Stephen O'Brien. However, shortly into proceedings, he found himself, for better or worse, very much in the spotlight:

"I have a young boy here. He suffered an impact to the head. Oh dear – it was a terrible impact … hit by a motorbike. He's dancing in here saying "*I'm not dead – I'm still alive*" and he's combing his hair in a teddy boy quiff. Is his name Tony? He's saying you used to comb his hair into this quiff. He's saying "*Comb my hair like yours*" and now he's saying you haven't got any windows! Can that be right? Do you understand?"

Andrew certainly did understand. Here was his little cousin, his uncle Brian's sadly missed son Tony, not just stating the obvious facts that could have been hooked out of newspaper articles by someone with unscrupulous intentions. He had brought in references that no one except Andrew could have known. So, of course the "no windows" statement made absolute sense. Andrew's house was in the throes of being remodernised. Just two days previously, the workmen had removed the windows.

And Tony was tickled pink.

"I had to come through …"

Dear Mum and Dad,

I had to come through to Andy the other day –

To let you know I love you so and I'm not far away.

I was worried so much that the grieving I see would never fade away.

So that's why I've come, to prove to you Mum, **I'm with you every day.**

So, please don't grieve, for I'm at ease and alive in every way.

People will say believe what you see but they don't understand

nothing can kill, perish or burn the eternal Spirit of Man.

So, as I have said, I love you all with living proof at first hand.

Please no more fears and no more tears …

I'll always hold your hand.

Tony x

Andrew McKellar

PATIENT TESTIMONIES

In their own words

CANCER

"Malcolm"

"In 1993 I had treatment for bowel cancer and it reoccurred as secondaries in 1999. They operated in 2000 and, after the operation, I was given nine months to live - tops. I went back to the medical profession for a six-month course of chemotherapy. They did the scans and there were several tumours scattered around the abdomen. My wife talked me into coming to see you. They were quite categorical that nine months was the best they could do for me."

"I came to you over eight weeks and then had a CT scan. The tumours had gone. They couldn't understand where they'd gone, as the type of chemotherapy I was receiving only shrinks tumours – it doesn't eradicate them. They would do another scan in three months' time to see. I also had a tumour on the lung. That's gone also. I kept coming to see you. I experienced heat – very warm at the contact points – a glow, and a feeling of well being. I didn't expect to be here. I was on borrowed time."

"Veronica"

"*I had ovarian cancer and pneumonia. I was diagnosed when I was given a hysterectomy. They found cancerous cells and a tumour as well. So they operated and took it out and then I developed pneumonia and was put in intensive care overnight. Then they transferred me to another hospital and after a couple of weeks I came home and came to see Andy. My husband had seen him before through a friend called Penny. He had sciatica and Andy cured him, basically in one session. He also cured Penny of M.E.*"

"*There were still some tumours left, which they found on the CT scan and some fluid. I felt intense heat – also a cooling going through the body like it was cleansing the body - and lots of colours. The recent scan revealed that the tumour on my liver had gone and the one on the right side had gone, plus the fluid there. I just have one small tumour left on the left side now. I had no reaction from the doctor that day but the nurse was gobsmacked. The nurse has opened her mind to healing. Andy saved my life. It's just phenomenal. To feel the heat and to feel relaxed. And to find out that he's curing you. They don't give you much hope. Doctors don't. I must admit my doctor at the hospital is very good. She's excellent – she listens to what you say. She takes notice of everything. Other doctors I've seen besides her don't. They're sort of matter of fact. They don't tell you an awful lot. You can ask them questions but I found it all out for myself. For ovarian cancer it's not good – about one in fifteen survive it. My blood count's been normal now for nine or ten months. The first time I came to see him it must have come down and it's carried on going down ever since. I don't think I'd be here today if it wasn't for Andy.*"

"Les"

"*In the mid-1990s I took my son to my local GP and I mentioned to him at the time about a growth on my arm. He didn't seem too concerned. I had to take my son back two or three times and mentioned it had grown and I asked him if I could have it removed. It turned into a one-centimetre cube with a black inner. He took it off for me, sent it off for biopsy and it came back as malignant. So he made an appointment for me to see a specialist at Southampton General Hospital. From there I went to Oddstock for wider excision where they took out an area around my wrist. I was told that they hoped they had caught it.*"

"*Six months later I had a lump under my left armpit and that turned out to be malignant again. I was in hospital for a couple of weeks for that operation and it was malignant melanoma – it had spread to my armpit. I was told I had two years. There are no treatments as such apart from chemotherapy and radiotherapy. Both ruin the time you've got and I was informed that it didn't help this particular form of cancer. I heard about Andrew McKellar and made an appointment. I saw Andrew once a week for quite a while and I believe he's helped me. Although I have been seeing a specialist every three months for two years and then once every six months (now I'm down to every year), she's a wonderful person but I would put it down to Andrew helping me a great deal. What Andrew does is put his hands on you and you'll feel a terrific amount of heat and you'll see colours – amazing. I'm very mechanically minded, so I was always asking questions – although his time's precious. You see purples and blues. I would go home exhausted and have to lie down. I still see Andrew. Once every two months he's good enough to slot me in. Because you can't see cancer – it's a way of fighting it. I had to do something and Andrew took it away.*"

"Dianne"

"In April 2002 I was diagnosed with having mesophelioma cells in the fluid of my lungs and then a month later I went into Southampton General Hospital and they confirmed it by taking a biopsy. It was a tumour in the lining. I was offered three options. One was to have a radical operation taking the lung away; or chemotherapy, or leave it alone. And where I am now I'm leaving it alone."

"Healing was like lifting a black sheet off. You could just start to live again and not think about your funeral. They'd only given me eighteen months to two years. You walk into Andrew's waiting room and it's the calmness – it's just lovely. The first time I came it was intense heat – almost like a water bottle – on the back. Very strong. Then he puts his hands over your eyes. I always see the reds and golds when he takes his hands away but sometimes, when they're left there, I can see sort of rainbow colours – greens and maybe ambers and violets and you just feel wonderful. You could stay there all day. Andrew's amazing. You can get your life back into something. I didn't think I would ever see my first grandchild being born but here I am with just a few weeks to go and it's just wonderful."

"Harry"

"After twenty-six years of suffering the terrible pain of renal colic, I went to see my consultant at Southampton General Hospital for the results of my fifty-fifth operation on my kidneys. He put my X-ray on the wall and said, I'm sorry. Both your kidneys are full of stones again  *and you've got prostate cancer. I said - well what are you going to do about it? He said there was nothing they could do. I was too old to have more operations; I'd had too many operations as it was; my heart was in a very bad state. He thought it would be fatal if he operated. I said, you must be able to do something. He said I'll put you on a scanner to try to get rid of the stones and we'll wait until the cancer spreads a little and then we'll go on to chemotherapy. I said thank you and went home. I then rang Andrew the next day."*

"On the Monday I had a telephone call and it was Andrew. He'd come home from India and picked my message up. We had a chat. He said to phone back in a month's time because he was so booked up. I said, I'm sorry, I won't be alive then. He rang me back with a cancellation the next day - would I like it."

"He brought his hands up my body slowly. When he got to my shoulders he just shook his hands and the pain had gone. He then asked me to move my neck, which I hadn't been able to do because I had arthritis so bad in the top of my spine that I hadn't been able to move my head for ages. He put his hands round my neck. After three or four minutes I was able to move my head around and do anything. I made arrangements to see him again and after seven weeks I had no more pain, no more stiffness of the neck and well I felt really relieved. A few weeks later I went to see my GP. She sent me for a blood test. A fortnight later the results came back and she was shocked. She said your blood is that of a young man!"

"Cath"

"*I'd been on HRT for a year and had never felt happy with it. They overdosed me with hormones and the side effect was breast cancer. I got swelling under my armpit in the lymph gland area and my right breast swelled to at least twice its normal size. I got awful pains in my chest and under my arms. Incredible pain – painkillers the whole time.*"

"*I felt as soon as you touched me all the emotion draining out of me. I felt instantly better. I felt floating. The pain had gone. By the time I got home the swelling had gone down and it's gradually continued to go down over the week. My right breast is the same size as my left now.*"

"*I also had a cyst under my knee on the right leg. The doctor said I'd have to put up with it. I could have it cut out but it would be a nasty operation and would leave a big scar. It was painful all the time. I had a healing session with you and that night I was in agony. But the next morning it had gone. The doctor couldn't believe it.*"

CHAPTER THREE

CHAPTER THREE

BAD HEALTH, BEDSITS AND BREAKING POINT

"Minds are like parachutes. They only function when open"

Andrew's childhood had presented him with more hurdles than most people would have to embrace in a lifetime. Thus far we have only focused on Andrew's spiritual childhood revelations. So it comes as a shock to learn from him that his younger years, right up to his mid-teens, were plagued by two serious and debilitating medical conditions.

"I had a very serious speech impediment. When I was two and a half years of age I was put in hospital because my father beat me up. It was a Saturday morning in the bedroom. Michael was in a cot and would rock the cot. The carpet had become pushed up against the door and because I couldn't open the door my parents got angry with me. They then asked me to flick up the latch on the window so that my father could climb in through the window. He then hit me with his belt but the buckle tore into the top of my leg. He threw me into their bedroom and locked the door. My leg was weak and wet and my hands were covered in blood. I was stitched up at hospital and from that day I had a serious speech impediment – a severe stammer – until I was fourteen."

Andrew's reaction to such treatment was to rebel against any form of authority. His father, he feels, was overly strict with him and so he became scared.

"I never stammered in front of my friends but in other public situations the stammer would start."

The speech impediment was to haunt Andrew until, as he puts it, he healed himself. It took him the better part of a year but cure it he did.

"I got rid of my speech problem completely. I had a problem with liking people. We were programmed to believe we were rubbish and I thought all people were like that. I decided that I didn't want it any more. I totally influenced its going. It took a year to rectify."

Today there remains no trace of it. And no sooner have we spent time talking about the trauma he feels his father caused him, we are moving swiftly on to an even more remarkable fact, finally diagnosed when Andrew was thirteen. Andrew, throughout his younger years, suffered with epilepsy.

"I also got rid of the epilepsy. I picked the drugs up in the kitchen one day. People without the condition can't appreciate what it's like. It's not the fits – it's this constant brain block – constant feeling of tiredness with the drugs – weakness in the muscles and nausea. I thought I didn't want to be like other people I knew with epilepsy where they had scars and teeth missing and jaws twisted through falling over. I was determined not to be like them – some ended up brain damaged. I threw the drugs in the bin at sixteen and my Mum phoned the doctor and I had to see him. He told me I would be in serious trouble by twenty – very serious trouble. But even on the drugs I had fits. I healed myself and, although I then had two fits in quick succession, I haven't had any more symptoms for over twenty-five years. Even then it wasn't straightforward. I wanted to drive. I approached the doctor and it was difficult to convince him that I was epilepsy-free. I had to fight for the right at twenty-nine."

But fight he did. Andrew McKellar wouldn't expect to do anything less.

By the time Andrew was seventeen he might have expected finally to escape the family influences he found so negative and that he'd come to dislike so much.

"I had an awful childhood. We never wanted for anything. We were fed and clean. But I was given absolutely no direction; no career advice. At seventeen I was kicked out by my father."

This abrupt ejection had actually been fuelled by problems Andrew suffered when he landed his first proper job. When he left school he got a job in a firm of sign printers. His father thoroughly approved. This would be Andrew's ticket to a good career, his own house, a car and the trimmings. But Andrew was living under the constant shadow of coping with epilepsy. He was told he would be on medication for life. And, within just three weeks of his apprenticeship, the fumes that were part and parcel of the job, made him so ill, he felt he had no choice but to leave. He actually agonised about doing so. He was artistic and had hoped that the environment would be good news. From where his father was standing, however, there was no way back. He saw Andrew's leaving as downright stupid and he simply withdrew any respect for his son.

"He never gave any of us any encouragement. He told me that the only job we would ever be good for would be sweeping the roads. We were programmed from an early age and I believed it myself."

Andrew was seventeen and on the streets.

He turned to drink. Weekends were the worst, downing beer until he was senseless just to get false confidence. I ask him if the boozing affected his spiritual "experiences". Looking back he thinks that they did "lapse" quite a bit but his spirit friends never gave him a tough time. They would never interfere.

By now he was reduced to living in old garages and woodland areas under bushes. He would prise the corrugated iron off old derelict buildings and sleep on the bare floorboards. He chose to go it alone. All in all he was on the streets for two to three years. Work was mostly painting and decorating (courtesy of friends with bedsits in need of a facelift). Signing on was out of the question because he had no fixed abode. His epilepsy was still ever present. He convinced himself he was just one of life's losers.

And then he met someone – a girlfriend. Together they got a council flat and Andrew recalls making a conscious decision to try better to fit in with society. Marriage followed, together with two children, Sarah and Andrew. Sadly, the marriage didn't last. Andrew is quick to take responsibility for its failure "… *because of my own insecurities back then."*

Andrew with daughter Sarah from his first marriage

Macolm "Jock" McKellar with his grandson Andrew Junior

*Andrew "Junior" – from his
first marriage*

Daughter Sarah

So it was back to the booze and staying out with friends at weekends. Andrew's view is that, as a couple, they simply ended up with no communication pattern. The split would mean that his younger child would choose to cut Andrew out of his life almost completely. He returned to bedsit land and describes that point in his life as rock bottom - a positively seedy life with nothing to look forward to. Nothing.

"I decided I couldn't carry on so I chose to take my own life. I took a rope on to Southampton Common to hang myself. I was desperate. Nothing was going to change my mind. But, as I made the final decision, I heard a voice 'Andrew – don't do this. You are one of a chosen few. There is much work for you to do'. I had a vision of masses of people coming towards me – literally clawing their way forward - saying 'Help me, Help me'. I was overwhelmed. I thought 'How can I help these people, when I can't even help myself?' But I didn't go ahead with the suicide. I carried on and eventually I was at a party one night and a chap came up to me. We started talking about life after death and he said to me he thought I should visit the spiritualist church."

Grove Road, Shirley in Southampton was the nearest spiritualist church and Andrew found himself there for the first time, installed in the back row, hoping he couldn't be seen. The medium on the platform had other plans it would seem. She pointed at Andrew and gave her opinion on much of his life to date.

"You've been through a heck of a lot as a young man. You've contemplated taking your life. Everything you've been through has been a test. Do you realise who you are? You have been born for a special purpose. You are going to become Britain's most famous healer. You are going to be the next Harry Edwards."

All of which was well and good but it did rather expose a gap in the McKellar spiritual education. He hadn't a clue who Harry Edwards was.

"You will be a healer. Within the next five years you'll have your own premises and you'll be approaching professional healing."

Andrew was twenty-three by now. It was winter; he was jobless; he was separated from a wife and children and, if he was honest with himself, he didn't really want to be bothered with healing people because he held practically no respect for the majority of people.

Andrew's depression can hardly have been helped by the standard of accommodation he was forced to accept. On the plus side, he was no longer living rough. The lifestyle makeover however was hardly radical. The stark truth was that all he could afford in the wake of his marriage failing was a sad and sorry attic room in a woefully neglected Victorian house. Southampton's Derby Road area had developed a reputation for attracting life's unfortunates but at least it was cheap. The house, once noble, was now a three-storey slum – a dodgy "Dunroamin" to a dubious selection of down and outs. Andrew viewed the attic room and felt he could probably make it habitable with a bit of elbow grease. He took it, gutted the room and gave it the planned lick of paint. It was, thankfully, a roof over his head and, as a first-time attic dweller, at least he could kid himself he was going up in the world.

It was shortly after taking up residence that he heard something odd. No one who took the room ever stayed in it for any length of time. The landlord had certainly not bothered to mention the room's reputation for weird things happening and a turnover of tenants that clearly betrayed a problem. Andrew had acquired a few spiritual books and was looking forward to reading one of them in his new room one night when he suddenly became aware of the sound of light breathing in the centre of his room. His first reaction was to suspect that he had down and out company under his bed. He checked it out. Nobody. By now, the breathing had become louder and Andrew was out of bed, checking the cupboard in the corner, looking in a wardrobe, even checking outside on the balcony to ensure there was no one there. All that continued to greet him was louder breathing. In utter frustration and bewilderment he decided to "have a word", as he puts it. The only thing he could think to blurt out on the spur of the moment was a shaky and melodramatic "*I recognise your presence.*" But it did the trick. The breathing was history. He admits to having felt rather frightened but, looking back, he now realises that this was just more consolidation of the spiritual ties, integral to his life. He was now fully adult and these psychic events were simply not disappearing. Andrew now believes that this was a time in his life when he was developing his own mediumistic talents. He was beginning to accept that he was far more "aware" and intuitive than most. He also suspected that he could probably do what the performing mediums in the spiritualist churches did. But his default was naturally to feel sceptical.

So, did he believe that the medium on the church platform, who predicted his life's destiny as healing, was at least genuine? For whatever reason, yes – he did. And, slowly, very slowly, life began to get just a bit better.

"PAPER"

If you set light to a piece of paper it shall burn from one end to the other.

If it is blown about in the wind, or rain pours down upon it, it will go out half burnt.

For God's love to burn through you, know that his hand holds you close to him; know that with his love and protection he will shelter you.

Always have ultimate faith in his omnipresence. And his love shall burn through you and cleanse you,

... and cleanse your soul with the fire of love.

Received in a meditative state
By Andrew McKellar

PATIENT TESTIMONIES

In their own words

BONES

"Robin"

"I had arthritis and my sister telephoned me in New Zealand to say there was a healer I should see in England. I was bullied into coming as I was very sceptical!"

"I had stiffness and deformities of the hand. Very swollen and my fingers were starting to curl. After the first healing session there was a dramatic difference. I hadn't been able to go up the stairs – I'd had to crawl up. I was on up to twelve pills a day, including steroids. I was blown out."

"I had five healing sessions. Now I can move my joints and the drugs have gone. That was the real bonus. I felt heat more than anything. It was like an electrical heat. My family felt I was a different woman getting off the plane. My Dad was there and sceptical until he saw me. Not any more."

"Eileen"

"*I suffered very badly with rheumatoid arthritis. It developed literally overnight and every day it was a real struggle to do everyday normal things. It not only affected me but also the family as well. I had a spa bath fitted; handles on plugs, an electric garage door and heavy, thick supports for the hands – night supports as well to keep my hands straight because they would lock over. It was impossible to straighten them up in the morning. I haven't worn them now since the first week I came to see you! I don't need injections any more. I don't need painkillers. I also suffered with a heart problem from birth - a rare syndrome – very rare. It didn't cause me too much of a problem until I was in my early teens and then I was given medication that didn't do anything at all. When I first came to you I didn't mention the heart problem. It came as some surprise to me when I went for an ECG and to see the cardiologist that the ECG was reading perfectly normally. I told him I was off any medication. We killed two birds with one stone!*"

"*It's been suggested that the arthritis is in remission. But patients in remission still have pain and take high doses of medication. I had remission when I had the disease and would feel better for some weeks but it would come back. Now I'm pain free.*"

"David"

"*I've had degeneration of my spine and suffered for eighteen months with the problem. I was a sceptic. A friend of mine had been greatly helped. I didn't know what to expect. I felt tremendous heat from your hands. I can't believe it. It's marvellous – fantastic. No pain at all – it's gone. My legs are fantastic now. What can I say? It was instant pain relief. I was gobsmacked - amazed. I've had five weeks off work with a great big bag of painkillers. I just got so cheesed off with it and I thought well, give it a go. There was nothing left to lose. My back's still warm. There were lights - coloured - mauvey, bright pink, blue. I wouldn't have believed it at first but seeing is believing.*"

"Edna"

"*I saw a chiropractor for a knee problem on four occasions, which cost me nearly two hundred pounds. When I finally got an appointment with you, after three treatments the pain had gone away. I am a post lady in Romsey. I didn't think I'd ever cope. It was a big struggle to do the job after twenty-five years.*"

"*I felt intense heat - it was in my body. I saw pinks, greys and blues. It calms me down. I panic over silly things. It keeps me steady. My nerves are better. I just feel like a new person!*"

"Ivor"

"I had a serious back complaint and was waiting to have an operation. Andrew didn't feel the operation was needed and hoped it could be cancelled after healing. After three healing visits I have seen the specialist, who says there is now no need to operate."

"I had the pain originally diagnosed as sciatica and it was treated as such. More than that, I was referred to Southampton General Hospital for tests and scans and a growth was diagnosed. Then a slipped disc. I was put on the emergency operating list. Two years waiting. I carried on with healing and felt penetrating heat on my leg and back areas."

"Pat"

"I've had osteo-arthritis since I was forty-two (about fourteen years). It had got so bad that I wasn't sleeping because my shoulders were so bad. My shoulders are really good now. What I didn't expect was that I'd have a lot more energy. I also suffer with seasonal affective disorder, which has gone, although it's now mid-winter!"

"I'm doing lots of things in the evenings. I'm sleeping better and I've joined a gym. I feel terrific warmth and sometimes see colours. Sometimes I feel I'm falling asleep. The colour is sometimes bright turquoise blue. It's made a marvellous difference to my life."

"Sue"

"I suffered with a serious spinal problem for over thirty-one years. I had been to the doctor, the osteopath, the chiropractor. For the last two years I've been going every week to the chiropractor. He can relieve it but by the end of the week it's back again. Since seeing you four days ago I have no pain. I've been skipping around the carpark. Everyone thinks I'm a total loon! No one can keep up with me. My muscles are relaxed. It's incredible. I was sceptical."

"You were easy to get on with. You just do it. I can't understand how quick it is. I would say to everyone come. The medical profession said there were a lot of people worse off than me. I'd get arthritis when I was older but tough. Stupidly, I accepted it. I feel confident and calm with you and a weight has been lifted off my shoulders. I felt a lot of heat. A calming, peaceful sense. I felt all my muscles relaxed. It was comforting. There were lots of colours – mainly green and purple and some gold."

"Terri"

"When I first came to see you I'd been having severe back problems for years since my early twenties. I'd been to chiropractors and osteopaths but when I first came I'd had a really bad flare-up. I'd been finding it really difficult to sit, lie down or walk for a period of about six months. When I came I was using a back-support – I took it everywhere. After two to three sessions with you I stopped using it. I use it at home if I'm going to be sitting for a very long time but I don't actually sit for long anymore because I can walk! I feel a lot better. On a scale of one hundred – ninety percent easily."

"I sleep a lot better. I used to dread going to bed because getting in and out of bed was like a military operation. The main thing I felt was intense heat and it stays with me most of the day. Not uncomfortably hot. I do see colours when you're on my back. I usually float out!"

"Trevor"

"*I had an injection when I was nineteen/twenty for a football injury. Since then the spinal problem got worse and came to a head when I was twenty-nine. I was advised to give up football by a doctor. I went to osteopaths and chiropractors. Before coming, on New Year's day I couldn't get out of bed. I tried to do some exercises on the floor. My wife said to see you. I was a bit sceptical but the doctors had said they couldn't do anything for me and the osteopath said I had a weakness there, so I came with an open mind.*"

"*I had seven to eight sessions and my spine feels fantastic now. I can even kick a ball around with the kids. I can do shoelaces up. I saw you twice for a frozen shoulder, which is very painful. The heat from your hands was unbelievable – very hot – sometimes hotter than other times. I see colours when you put your hands over my eyes – purples and all sorts of colours. The amazing thing – especially for my back – was that it freed up straight away. I would say to anyone - It can take time. If it doesn't get cured first time don't give up until you reach that one hundred percent.*"

"Ian"

(Ian's mother is speaking)

"At age seven Ian was quite active. He enjoyed all sports and he danced. Then one night he couldn't stand. We whipped him up to the hospital and they found that the cap had slipped off of the knee bone. They put him in traction and we got him back home three days later. This was on a regular basis. Then he started walking on tiptoes. It didn't bother Ian. It bothered other people because it wasn't the natural way to walk. We took him back to hospital and he was in and out for about three years and they really still didn't know what was wrong. They were testing for M.S. - everything."

"About the sixth stay at the hospital they discovered in an X-ray that he had a variation of the femur. They gave him painkillers. It stayed dormant and they said to keep giving him painkillers. The hip would move on they said; the deterioration would get worse and then he would need a hip replacement. He saw you for healing and the doctors are very surprised that he's off the painkillers now."

(Ian speaking)

"During healing your hands were very hot and when you put your hands over my eyes I saw orange colours and bright lights."

CHAPTER FOUR

CHAPTER FOUR

BEGINNING TO HEAL AND SAI BABA

"The greatest pleasure in life is doing what people say you cannot do"

There was nothing for it. Andrew had to get hold of a book about Harry Edwards and actually read it. He did so and discovered a remarkable tale - a man, who performed the most astonishing healing feats from his early awareness of healing powers in the 1930s right up to his death in 1976. This was a human being, who had devoted his life to sharing his healing gift with those in need of comfort and cure; a man, who established an internationally-renowned healing sanctuary in a beautiful part of Surrey as far back as 1946. There are innumerable books on and by Harry Edwards. Reading one was enough to convince Andrew that the ability to heal was a precious and extraordinary gift.

The healer who really inspired Andrew to do something serious with his gift however was the late Ted Fricker, who had lived and practised in London.

"I had an uncanny pull towards him. He'd had similar experiences in his childhood. He wasn't religious. Later in life – two to three years ago – I left my body and met him. He took my hand and said 'Andrew you are destined to do this work for the rest of your life, just like I was'. I began to take my path seriously."

He started to attend the spiritualist church in Shirley on a regular basis and that's where he met Rose, who took him under her wing. They acquired a flat together in Millbrook not far from the church and remained together for the better part of ten years. Rose herself experienced just a little in terms of spiritual experiences. Now, however, Andrew felt he had some space to develop. He now found getting employment that much easier – not sticking at the work in any long-term fashion but generally making ends meet. He worked for a paint firm, social services and a boat mast manufacturer.

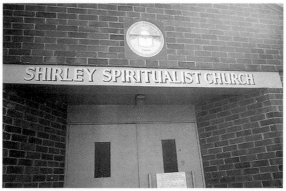

Shirley Spiritualist Church, Grove Road, Southampton

Grove Road Spiritualist Church where Andrew received the life-changing healing destiny message

Inexplicable paranormal activity continued to serve as a constant reminder to Andrew that he was not alone. For whatever reason, when disturbances occurred Andrew always imagined first that he had burglars. It was only ever after discounting human intruders that, each time, the penny would drop.

Andrew describes just how terrifying these activities could be. Rose and he were in the throes of having their flat modernised. In bed one night he suddenly heard what he thought was someone outside his bedroom door "kicking the hell out of it". He dived out of bed, arming himself with a piece of the workmen's wood conveniently discarded on the floor. The landing was empty but the "intruder" was clearly now in the bedroom opposite. Rose and Andrew's possessions had gone into large boxes for the duration of the home improvement works and were all in the bedroom concerned. Andrew could hear boxes being scraped across the floor, boxes being placed in other boxes, boxes thudding against the floor. By now, anger had replaced fear. Someone was out of order with their possessions and in their home, uninvited. Andrew was going to take them on. He kicked open the door, flicked on the light switch and, Sumo-like, prepared to tackle the noisy interloper. Except his opponent was missing. Andrew was greeted with boxes moved higgledy-piggledy across the floor. Whatever had shifted them had clearly got bored. The only way out was the bedroom door. And Andrew had been standing in it.

I ask Andrew if he knows why it happened. Was there a message in such anti-social, unsubtle and tantrum-like behaviour? Andrew hasn't a clue. But he did make the bedroom into his healing room. Just to be friendly.

And heal he did. For England. The Southampton Daily Echo newspaper had been featuring Andrew's success stories. People were obviously reading it. They came in force, always keen to receive the healing energy but often not so keen to dig deep into pockets when it came to donations. Andrew had to maintain a part-time job as well. And he was about to learn the first lesson of healing. Control.

He had just finished a back-to-back, full day of healing. He remembers it was a beautiful late afternoon and Rose was on her way down the maisonette stairs clutching a watering can. On the point of relaxing, he turned around. And hit the floor. Something was wrong. This wasn't his old epilepsy. This was something altogether different. He felt drugged.

"I managed to crawl to the bedroom and collapsed into bed – boots and all. I was under the continental quilt and nothing was going to shift me.

And then suddenly I could hear breathing by my right ear. I was so scared I just couldn't open my eyes. I was then aware of a physical form and I remember reciting The Lord's Prayer to myself, even though I'm not religious in that sense, and thinking – Andrew, what a hypocrite you are."

"Then a pair of hands literally came through the quilt and on to my lower abdomen. I could feel the warmth of the fingers. They remained there for a few seconds and then slowly moved up in stages until they reached my throat. By now, I was reaching a panic state and, as if it had realised, an audible voice said: 'We are not here to harm you my child – we are here to help you. You must control the healing energies. You must not overwork your own energies. You could slip into a coma and die'. It had lasted no more than a couple of minutes. I then fell asleep and awoke at 8.00 the next morning. Rose had tried to wake me but all attempts had failed. I had slept for over fourteen hours."

"BETTY"

Much of Andrew's healing revolved around everyday illnesses. Patients would attend for healing and return, if necessary, over an agreed period of time. Betty had been an elderly patient, whom Andrew had treated successfully for arthritis. She had then been diagnosed with lung cancer. Out of the blue one Saturday, Andrew received a telephone call from Betty's daughter Diane. It was not good news. Betty was in hospital. The family had been summoned to her bedside. The hospital staff were muting "an hour". Diane wondered if Andrew could possibly come to the hospital "just to help Betty pass over".

What greeted Andrew was a highly distressing sight. Betty was barely conscious but, at least, he felt she knew him and was able to smile a little. He knelt down and held her hand. He placed his hands on her chest, resigned to the fact that this must be Betty's time to go.

But Betty didn't check out of life. A week later she checked out of hospital. And her chest scan revealed that her lung cancer had also gone A.W.A.L. Betty lived on happily for another fifteen years. Later she told Andrew that after he had left that night she had felt an urgent pulling on her left-hand side. She was convinced that this was the power of death. Then she had felt an even stronger pulling on her right-hand side, as if Andrew were physically pulling her back to life. Leaving would obviously have been impolite!

~~~

Healing worked. Everyday, Andrew was using his gift to alter the balance of people's lives. He was guardian of an absolutely awesome, life-changing energy. And, most importantly, he had established himself as a healer.

It wasn't all plain sailing however. To assist his progression he attended a development circle, recommended by the Grove Road spiritualist church. Whilst it gave him some insight, he became disturbed that people within the circle weren't really getting results. The church made it plain that he wasn't welcome. His criticism wasn't welcome. They were shutting the door. From Andrew's point of view, it wasn't a loss. He didn't want, or intend, to do the spiritualist "platform" work. His experiences in the congregation had not convinced him that the performers' level of mediumship (for the main part) was much good. He found himself making enemies and believes that there was jealousy towards him because he had started to be featured in the local press.

"I don't need people or religion – apart from Sai Baba, whom I first went to see fifteen years ago in India."

Indian guru Bhagavan Sri Sathya Sai Baba, I will learn, is held to be a spiritual phenomenon of the highest order by his millions of followers throughout the world. Now aged over seventy-seven, he is deemed by his followers to be God Incarnate, his name a combination of "Truth" (*Sathya*) and "Divine Mother and Father" (*Sai Baba*). Andrew is firm in his conviction that Sai Baba is a true miracle worker. So, when Andrew matter of factly confirms that Sai Baba "visits" him regularly, without actually leaving India, one finds oneself simply drinking the information in. Any debate about how, why, when and how often would simply seem out of place.

"*A friend introduced me and said come to India. I didn't hesitate and it was brilliant. I experienced quite a bit. Ever since I've had visitations from him personally. I visually see him manifest – he appears to me in dreams, in English. Plus I sense him. You have to experience him personally. Books and videos aren't the same as first-hand. I was in the front row for my first visit and felt instant recognition. He appeared one night in my doorway – it threw me out of bed. I grabbed a bit of paper. The voice said:*

'*I am the stem of the flower; you are my petals;*
I give you strength to cling to me;
to grow in all strength and to flourish in all beauty;
take the water from the stem;
the water is my love;
call upon me and I shall guide and protect you'

I try to keep to it."

Spiritual leader "Bhagavan Sri Sathya Sai Baba".
Andrew's spiritual teacher, whom he sees as a true friend

Andrew maintains that he has made a conscious decision not to be a churchgoer. Instead he prefers to live his life as spiritually as he possibly can. His calling is to help as many people as feasible through the power of unconditional love. Of the thousands of Sai Baba sayings, he has two treasured ones, which certainly seem very appropriate for an individual with Andrew's gift and outlook on life:

"The hands that serve are holier than the lips that pray."

"If you help just one person in need, this act becomes holier than a church filled with a thousand people."

He has obviously read much on the subject of world religion and philosophies, believing that most faiths encounter problems simply because they see only one way – theirs. He believes the diamond analogy perfectly illustrates why religions are inspired in the first place and what lies behind them:

"The easiest way to understand is symbolically. Imagine a diamond in the sky – the diamond has many facets. And from each facet, if there is light coming from behind it, comes a ray of light. Each religion is connecting to its one, individual facet. They give it a name and a form: Allah, Buddha, Krishna, Jesus etc … They are only seeing their one facet. They can't see the other facets and consequently they're not seeing the oneness – the omni-present force of the universe. They all connect to exactly the same source at the end of the day."

When one looks ahead to Andrew's 2003 healing sanctuary, it is impossible to miss the enormous importance that he places upon Sai Baba's influence. There are three beautifully crafted statues of the guru - gifts from the sculptor wife of one of Andrew's patients, whom, he says, he cured of leukaemia. As if two Sai Baba busts aren't gratitude enough, the third statue is life-sized – a glorious celebration of saffron robes and big hair, dominating the private healing room and ever present. Andrew had experienced a vision several years before of a life-sized statue of the spiritual leader, so as a gift it was wonderfully appreciated but as a surprise he had just expected it to become a reality. And I myself do not escape the great guru's wisdom. As Andrew and I liaise on the content of this book, I am constantly reassured by Andrew that "*the book is already in the pen.*"

"*I seek advice frequently from Sai Baba. If he is able to give me an answer, he will come. I have been to India to see him now three times. The strength, guidance, wisdom and understanding he gives me are immeasurable. He did actually tell me that we were going to buy this house and foretold problems …*"

And, later, when I am searching through the many hours of filmed healing testimonies Andrew has gathered over the years, I stop at the interview he has done with a highly grateful patient, a lady who knew nothing about Andrew's devotion to Sai Baba:

"FREDA"

"*Before healing I was suffering with spondylitis of the spine. It was in my neck and very painful. I had to wear a collar and was on painkillers. It just made my life a misery. I couldn't move my neck either way and it was getting a bit awkward for driving because I couldn't turn my neck. In bed I would get a kind of vertigo and if I went to turn over I would feel sick and it was a misery. The first time I came to see you I felt these two clicks in the back of my neck and went home and threw the collar away. It's been absolutely brilliant. I experienced intense heat and I felt the clicks and since then there has been no re-occurrence and I am off the medication. I experienced bright lights but another time I experienced a long tunnel, which was very beautiful with shiny grey bricks. At the end of the tunnel there was this little figure in orange with black bushy hair. I didn't realise at the time that this was Sai Baba. I have prayed to him and thanked him every day ever since.*"

Andrew views Sai Baba not just as his spiritual inspiration and teacher. He genuinely believes that the guru is his chief protector. A guardian angel, if one likes, ever watchful to keep Andrew safe. There are three stories Andrew tells – all car-related and the first one really rather amusing.

"Sai Baba appeared to me in a dream. I was walking up a garden path and putting a key into a house door. As I turned it, a vehicle drew up. It was a bright orange transit van with 'Sai Baba Auto Repairs' on the side! I walked back down the path and there he was, in the driving seat, winding down the window and beaming at me. Then the window went back up and he drove off. Next morning I was really worried about going out because of the dream. However, I had to and while I was driving on the motorway, my master brake cylinder went. Suddenly, travelling in the outside lane at full speed, I had no brakes. I pumped away and finally slowed the car down. I was very shaken. When I got home, I rang a car repair firm and they came out to my house. When it arrived, it was a transit van, which said 'Stephen Brown Auto Repairs' down the side. A bright orange transit van!"

On another occasion, Andrew awoke one morning with a startling vision of a car hitting another car. What was worse, he felt sure that the car hit was his. Once again, he was so convinced that this was a real warning, he decided to stay in all day. However, later in the day he had no option but to go out. He stopped his Mini by traffic lights at Southampton's Ocean Village and then describes how he knew he was going to be hit from behind at the traffic lights on red. He glanced in his rear view mirror and saw nothing. But the second glance up revealed a Cavalier car travelling at a speed which clearly was too fast:

"He hit me hard and, literally, as it was happening, I called out to Sai Baba to help me. When I got out of my car I saw the front of his car was badly damaged; I also saw the look of astonishment on his face. The back of my Mini was completely untouched."

The third story involves not just Andrew in his car but his two young children as well. He is convinced that had Sai Baba not been looking out for him, they all wouldn't be here today to tell the tale:

"In those days I drove a Metro. We were at Cobden Bridge in Bitterne in Southampton. It's a large and very busy junction and we were at red lights, turning back to green. Suddenly I heard a voice in the car from

*nowhere. It said 'Andrew - Slow down!' – twice. I had been accelerating
away from the lights but I braked and trickled across. The cars behind me
must have thought it was very strange. Until they saw the red Porsche
come out of nowhere at breakneck speed. It had jumped the other traffic
lights and, had I not held back, we would have been hit at speed."*

*The famous 'vibhuti' sacred ash – which manifests on Sai Baba
pictures throughout the world*

~~~

However, fascinating as these stories are, for the moment we are
concentrating on how Andrew McKellar started practising his healing. I
ask him if he can remember his very first treatment session. The trouble
is, just like his Sai Baba anecdotes, there have been so many wonderful
stories – the list just tumbles out:

"A lady came to me recommended by a friend of a friend. She was suffering from a huge tumour in her stomach. I cured her. The local Southampton Advertiser press got involved. I worked on friends and relatives. My Mum had had a large cyst on her wrist for over forty years. Within three to four weeks it had gone. My father had a heart attack and he was having difficulty getting around. I cured him. My Mum's friends started to ask to see me so that I could 'see off' their arthritis and aches and pains."

"One of my first big successes was when a lady, who was a member of the spiritualist church, asked me to see an elderly eighty-three year old friend in Southampton General Hospital, dying of bronchial pneumonia, even if I could just ease her suffering. Her tongue was hanging out. The nurse looked at me to indicate that there was no hope. Within three days she was out of bed cracking jokes. She lived for quite a few years afterwards and even moved house. I also treated the spiritualist church lady's husband for a throat cyst he needed an operation for. Two sessions were enough. I did a documentary for the TV about M.E. sufferers. People were banging the door down to get in to see me."

Perhaps one of Andrew's proudest healing experiences relates to his own father – the man who had perpetually doubted his son's stories, dismissing them as pure fiction. Malcolm McKellar first suffered a stroke and then a heart attack. The illnesses left him permanently weakened, eternally slipping pills under his tongue and generally incapable of walking more than a few yards without having to rest up. Andrew offered his father a series of healing sessions and, at last, his father had to concede, Andrew's healing channelling was working its wonders. It was a hugely significant time for father and son. What had been a bitter, unhealthy relationship historically began to change. And very much for the better.

Malcolm McKellar had begun to trust his son as he had never appeared to before. Andrew's father was clearly very proud of his boy. Perhaps a little late in the day but Andrew bears no grudges. He remembers his father saying to him, in sheer gratitude for his healing help: *"Andrew, I was your father once; now you're mine."* He asked Andrew for his opinion on how long he might "have left". Andrew felt he would go on for years, assuming that he give up the dreaded cigarettes that had probably hastened the heart problems in the first place.

And then, at a time when Andrew's life was beginning to find the balance and harmony it had lacked for so much of his life, his father decided to part from his mother, returning to London where he had been born, and finding somewhere to live in Camden. Thankfully, their relationship would remain much more "bonded" until his father's death several years later. Friends would be recommended by his father to travel down from London to receive Andrew's healing. Faith indeed.

Taking stock, Andrew had fulfilled the predictions he had received in his earlier years. There he was, in a position to share his healing gift with people in desperate need. Suddenly he wasn't having to look for work. The work was finding him. He was in demand. And he wanted to be there. For people.

WAVE OF THE HAND

As the devotees wait for him
to appear from the ashram
as the sun goes dim,
as the Indian sun goes down,

... he appears from his ashram
in his orange gown.

A glow around him
to light up the place,
a loving smile on every face.

As he moves out through the crowds,
blessing people as he moves round,

... a twirl, a flick - from his splendid hand
vibhuti* appears at his command.

All the people seated around,
numbers run in thousands
as they're scattered around.
As he glides along, touching some heads

... a twirl of his wrist, the vibhuti sheds.

The healing he gives, the smile on his face,
the power of his eyes so filled with grace.
"I know you all" we hear him say
"not even a thought can go astray"
"I shall be there in your hour of need
to guide and protect you, you shall see.
Just one thought to me, a cry for help,

... Baba is there to help you out"

21 January 1990
Andrew McKellar

* vibhuti: sacred ash, manifested by Sri Sathya Sai Baba and given to devotees as a
sign of grace and healing

PATIENT TESTIMONIES

In their own words

ACCIDENTAL INJURIES

"Audrey"

"In 1991 on a very dark, wet evening I slipped on a step on to a patio. I skidded and damaged all my thigh muscles. I had ten days in hospital and then for the next four to five years I was attending hospital. I had every kind of treatment that they could think of and, in the end, I decided it was a bit futile to keep going. So then I thought about healers and I didn't know who to go to or where to go and I wanted to get the right person. Then I saw Andrew's article and this was after eight years of pain and sleepless nights and I knew immediately when I saw it that he was the person I had to go to."

"From his hands there is terrific heat. When I first came it wasn't so warm. It's a very peaceful feeling and I always go home and have about five hours sleep afterwards. And I'd like to say that right from the very first day I saw Andrew I slept. The first night I slept twelve hours and then my husband woke me up. I hadn't slept for eight years. It was wonderful."

"My condition today is completely normal. I can do anything I want to do. Whereas before, if I went into town, within half an hour I'm looking for the bus, now I can stay all day – I can run for the bus even! And it's wonderful – I can go out every day instead of about once a week. He changed my life."

"June"

"My wrists were badly damaged in a car accident. Both wrists took the impact of the steering wheel. I had weakness for seven years. I couldn't lift things. I was told it was Repetitive Strain Injury. I've been on various drugs for it – they've actually given me strengthening exercises. I had an operation on one wrist. Cosmetically I disliked the lump it left and always wore long sleeves."

"After my first healing session I could feel the difference just through picking up the kettle and full saucepans. Now I can carry shopping bags! Just brushing my hair was difficult. The movement before was too much for anything."

"I have been back to the doctor. He was amazed. Now I've got no scars. I felt tremendous heat and on my back a tingling sensation - very hot. I saw bright blue and purple colours."

"Nolene"

"I had an accident at twenty and suffered whiplash in my neck. The last few years it seems to have got worse. My neck used to lock. I had terrible pain down to my elbows. It was really quite sore and cracking in the morning. The doctors said it was posture – I knew it wasn't. Healing gave me tremendous heat – beautiful different colours. I felt as if you'd taken the plug out. Tremendous calm and a good night's sleep. I only came for a couple of weeks. Now it's all gone. I see bright reds, yellows and mauve - different colours each week. You've helped me in other ways too."

"Tessa"

"*I had brought friends along for healing and had seen Andrew fifteen years earlier. I had a head-on collision with a car when I was seventeen and had a neck problem. I had continuous problems, seeing the doctor and physiotherapist and having all sorts of treatments, which didn't work. A friend had had very bad arthritis and she asked me what was different about her one day and I said – God your fingers are straight! She said you want to go and see Andrew with your neck, which I did. I came to you and after one session I was fine. I did come to you again but the problem had gone. I've been OK since and that was fifteen years ago!*"

"*I felt tremendous heat from your hands and I saw lots of different colours – bright. The heat felt as if it was going from one side of my neck to the other. I was so miserable before. Whenever I got tired, my neck hurt and I had to lie down. That's just disappeared and I've been great.*"

CHAPTER FIVE

CHAPTER FIVE

"HELPERS"

**"The goal of science is to build better mousetraps
The goal of nature is to build better mice"**

Up to this stage, whenever Andrew had mentioned his "voices" and "visitors" in conversation with me, it had been to illustrate just how incongruous his childhood was and to stress how strong an influence "non-earthly" presences and messages were on his life's own choices.

But, with the advent of his practical healing career, came a whole new spiritual energy. Andrew McKellar was not having to face his "hands on" future on his own. Whilst living with Rose and establishing himself with an increasing number of patients, he was aware that he was receiving medical assistance from a qualified doctor. This was a medical man with experience of treating a whole range of medical conditions, a scientifically trained individual with his own spiritual "surgery" – a Doctor Williams (deceased). Sensed, heard but never seen. Until, one night lying in bed, Andrew decided the time had come to meet him properly.

DR WILLIAMS

"I thought he was a burglar. Dr Williams appeared solid at the end of the bed one night. He was a tall, slim and immaculately dressed man with what I'd describe as a very peaceful face. He had a long, black cloak with a low top hat. Very Victorian era I would say. I had been hearing his name frequently and decided that I would ask him to appear. After about forty-five minutes of mentally requesting that he show himself, I said out loud – Are you there? And that's when he appeared. He didn't say a word. But then he started walking down the side of my bed and even I was frightened! I hid under the covers. When I re-emerged he had vanished."

Dr Williams is now a regular, professional spirit helper for Andrew. And it isn't just Andrew who sees him. Some patients have reported seeing this type of figure in their own bedrooms and even the kitchen. Patients have also commented on his presence in Andrew's healing room.

It would be about five years after meeting Dr Williams that another spirit doctor would report in to help – a doctor with a more definite specialisation – a Dr Cotton.

DR COTTON

"*I was introduced to a psychic surgeon - Dr Cotton. I had an experience where I left my body and went to a room. I sat down in a reclining chair and Dr Cotton wanted to speak with me. He was much more of a modern-day person in his appearance – normal shirt – no white gown. It was only several moments after he started speaking that I noticed he was speaking to me without moving his lips. He explained that in the spirit world you don't have vocal chords. You adapt to mind communication. My first words were to ask his name. He replied 'Names are unimportant – it's the work which is important', but then he told me he was Dr Cotton. For me it was instant recognition. I knew that I had known him from a previous existence. He then began operating on a young girl – a girl with a growth on her forehead. I actually found it rather unpleasant to be watching the procedure but he told me I had to watch because I'd be doing it one day. He's the tumour man.*"

OTHERS

And it doesn't stop with the duo of doctors. Andrew stresses that he has a variety of additional helpers. We talk about his North American Indian guides and, when I ask him if he can give me examples of who they might be and where they lived, he smiles and says by all means but it will take forever. We agree he might as well have a Reservation full!

Perhaps the most fascinating helper story is the one he mentions about a little girl who sometimes "comes" – Linda Martel. Andrew had read a fascinating and inspiring book about Linda. She had died of kidney failure aged only five in the Channel Islands the year before Andrew himself was born. Despite her life being so short, it had been a remarkable one. A spina bifida sufferer herself, she had built a reputation for being able to heal the sick, reaching out from the pram to touch and heal people from a very early age. Andrew wrote to her mother Eileen to tell her how impressed he was with the story. He sent her some press cuttings and video material relating to his own healing work and the two corresponded for a while. He received a photograph of Linda from her mother.

Not long afterwards, Andrew would learn from some of his patients that they had seen a little girl in his healing room, often sitting on their laps. And then, Andrew saw Linda Martel himself. He was entering his healing room one day and watched the outline of the little girl building up in front of him. The image was at first transparent but gradually took on a much more normal, physical appearance. It was the little girl in the photograph. Andrew is absolutely certain that Linda Martel is helping him with his healing:

"I've seen her once. Lots of patients have seen her. She died in 1961 and was a healer in Guernsey. She died aged five years. I have been in contact with her mother. Linda used to reach out of her cot from two years of age to heal people. She helps me with my healing sometimes."

HELPING OTHERS ... FROM A DISTANCE

Andrew was about twenty-nine when he finally realised how precious his "out-of-body" experiences could be. Prior to this, he had always been intrigued by the process and interested in his ability to, as he puts it, travel "astrally". However, a telephone call out of the blue from a nurse was to provide him with a sequence of events, which in turn would furnish him with an altogether higher level of understanding.

The nurse in question had been recommended to contact Andrew on behalf of a lady she was nursing. Her patient "Anne" had been suffering with leukaemia. The nurse was at pains to confirm that Anne was not open to any belief in anything. Her condition was terminal. She was a widow in her fifties, on her own and, by the sound of it, desperately ill physically and depressed and suspicious mentally. That aside, the nurse persuaded Anne to visit Andrew McKellar in Southampton later that month.

Anne's first visit to Andrew was, he describes, hard work. He sensed "*a huge barrier between us*". However, he also felt enormous compassion for this weak and lethargic woman and recognised that he was undoubtedly her last hope. Anne attended Andrew's healing sanctuary for over two months, accompanied initially by her nurses but, later when she was feeling considerably stronger, under her own steam.

Andrew, by now, felt that they had formed much more of a bond. Anne was seeing results at last. She had heaps more strength and vitality. She was recommending others to Andrew – praise indeed. She looked forward to continuing to come. In short, she had come to trust him. She had a new lease of life.

Unfortunately, Anne's progress was cut tragically short when she was caught in stormy weather, getting soaked through in the rain. Andrew witnessed her immediate decline and remembers that he then realised that hope was running out. He is the first to recognise that there are simply some patients for whom life on earth will terminate sooner than they might have hoped. No amount of healing will save someone whose time is simply "up".

From this point, events moved frighteningly quickly. One of the nurses telephoned Andrew to ask if he would visit Anne. He travelled up North to her home, accompanied by a friend. Up to this point, he had no idea what type of background Anne came from. However, when he found himself on what he thought was a long road, only to discover it was her driveway, he realised that this was an extremely wealthy woman. A maid greeted them at the front door and showed them up a sweeping staircase to Anne's bedroom. What greeted Andrew was an extremely shocking sight. Anne was lying in bed, much weakened and withered – clearly nearing the end of her life. Andrew gave her healing, purely to provide her with calmness and reassurance, kissed her on the forehead and said his goodbyes. This time, he knew, was a last goodbye.

A few months after Anne's death, Andrew had another of his out-of-body experiences. Within a matter of minutes of travelling up through the ceiling of his home and at tremendous speed over roofs and treetops, he found himself standing outside a remarkably familiar oak front door. It led to an equally familiar spiral staircase and, finally, what was indisputably his late patient Anne's bedroom door. From this point on he recalls that progress was fraught. It took him three attempts to get through the door into the bedroom. Having done so, he was greeted by the figure of Anne sitting alone, looking stressed and extremely angry. *"What are you doing here Andrew? Why hasn't anybody come to see me?"*

It was only at this stage that Andrew believes he fully understood the synchronicity of the events surrounding his relationship with this patient. He suddenly realised that the whole scenario of that initial telephone call from the nurse, followed by Anne's coming to see him originally, was to alleviate her suffering. Not just her physical, degenerative medical suffering but her less obvious, utter grief at having no faith in anyone at all. Andrew believes that her own late relatives knew that her physical death would leave her earth-bound for many years because of her inability to trust. And, indeed, Anne had remained alone in her bedroom, unable to accept she was dead. Stranded and outraged.

In response to Andrew's *"Anne, no one's come to see you because you've died"*, Anne hit back with a *"Don't talk so stupid"* rebuff. But Andrew persevered, watching Anne incredulously, somewhat pitifully pinching her arms and stressing to him that she could feel herself. Of course she was alive. Suddenly, Anne pointed at a wall and said *"I'm not going with them."* All Andrew could see was a blank wall. However, as he stared at it, he saw a prick of light, expanding to become a swirling mass of white light. It formed a tunnel and Andrew saw outlines of people. Turning back to Anne he urged her to go towards the people waiting for her. Her reluctance was overbearing. But Andrew persevered. She knew he could trust her. She knew he only wanted to help her. He was the one person she had learned to trust at the end of her life:

"*Her face softened. The worry and fear drained and she walked into the tunnel. She didn't look back.   Not a word to me. She didn't even say thank you!*"

But you can see from Andrew McKellar's face that he sees the experience as one of his great triumphs, and a wonderful learning curve. And that's what counts.

BAREBACK

*I ride bareback in the black hills,
the black hills of my ancestral tribe.*

*I ride bareback in the black hills
as my heart beats to memories of pride.*

*I feel the spirit of the sun
that shines through way up high.*

*I reminisce over my people
as tears well in my eyes.*

*A proud race of Indians, we once were,
at peace with the spirit of life*

*A proud race of Indians – yes, we were,
filled with the spirit of light.*

*Peace in the tribes, peace on the land -
the spirit of life lending a hand*

*At one we felt, peace in the mind -
At one we felt, filled with pride.*

*Our teepees stood tall, our fires glowed bright,
finding the love of our spiritual light.*

*I feel inside the strength we planned -
I feel my ancestors roaming this land.*

*Sometimes I hear their ghostly calls -
my ancestors calling the chants of old.*

*I sit on a rock, I call out loud -
I ask the Great Spirit*

To make us proud.

Andrew McKellar

PATIENT TESTIMONIES

In their own words

OTHER CONDITIONS

Scleroderma – Poliomyelitis – Cataract – Gynaecological Problems – Migraine – Spinal Spondylosis – Throat Lump - Frozen Ankle – Psoriasis – Asthma – Endometriosis

---

"Cathy"

"I had scleroderma. It's an auto-immune disease like rheumatoid arthritis. They don't know why it starts but the immune system starts to attack itself. You get very painful joints and damage to organs. I have damage to the lungs and digestive system. In effect the organs don't work effectively. I was diagnosed nine years ago and I'm monitored. There's no cure. So it's anti-inflammatories and various medications for the stomach - all of which have side effects of their own. A young girl I go to for massage told me about you. I thought, what have I got to lose?"

"I've had a new lease of life. My GP had recommended I shouldn't work anymore. It was hard to get through from one end of the day to the next. I was having trouble swallowing. I had hospital admission because of a stomach problem. In the months I've been seeing you I've gone from strength to strength. Six months ago I had to have a lung function test. It had significantly improved. I told the doctor and he said in my situation he would have done exactly the same. The heat is the primary thing with me. Sometimes I see colours. Afterwards I feel very calm and relaxed. Don't worry about why it works. It works! That's all that matters."

"Lyn"

"*I suffered from polio from about the age of five and had to go into hospital for major operations because the polio had left me with very weakened muscles. The operations managed to keep me going through the years but about four to five years ago the leg deteriorated to such an extent that it was quite frightening. And it frightened me mentally, physically and across the whole board. I went to the hospital and all I got from the specialists was - you've had polio - there's not much we can do. When I asked about the deterioration and how quickly it had deteriorated, they said – that's to be expected because you're an old polio. The muscles in the foot had gone. There was no life in them and they told me that once they had died they'd never come back. I was to the point of despair because my whole life had fallen apart. My leg had packed up but the pain in the leg at night would feel like a lump of raw meat in respect that the pain was burning – the leg was useless.*"

"*I was on crutches and the hospital's only answer was to try a calliper. It absolutely broke my heart. I did not want it. There had to be something else. The hospital made me feel as though I was another number — a useless person. They did their best. When I came to see you I couldn't walk across the room. You were so confident that the healing would help. I wasn't sure and you were so positive that I thought I've got nothing to lose. There is no one that can help me. I just placed it all over to you. After the second session I knew the leg would come back to life. It affected my family because I was so depressed. My daughter was frightened by my mental state. The healing has opened up my life. Friends and family cannot believe the difference in me!*"

"Peter"

"*I was having difficulty with looking at television particularly and had been warned by the optician that I had eye problems. My doctor diagnosed a cataract in my left eye. I suppose I'd lost about twenty-five per cent of the vision in my left eye, which didn't please me at all. I had brought my wife to you for healing and as we were leaving you cupped your hand over my eye for twenty seconds or so. I noticed there was an improvement and the next morning I removed a 'film' from the corner of my eye. Then I had a full healing session with you. I felt the heat and a sense of relaxation and deep peace.*"

"*I have regained full sight in the eye. I went back to the optician and he said he could find no cataract problem. It's better vision in my left eye now than in my right!*"

"Sue"

"*Three years ago I had a sterilisation done and ever since I've been suffering with really bad pains in my groin and side. I carried on for three years and it got so bad that the doctor said I would have to see a gynaecologist. I was appalled by the way I was treated. He told me I had to have a hysterectomy and I had a week to think about it.*"

"*I was in a lot of pain. I was taking painkillers, on and off for three years. When I first came I was always feeling sick and had really bad stomach pain. As soon as your hands were on my stomach I felt a very hot sensation - burning. It was a comfortable feeling. The sickness disappeared there and then. The second session I was complaining to you that I had pains in my groin still and by the third or fourth session they had completely gone. My back was bad. I'd been off work – I work in a nursing home. That's fine now – I'm back at work. I'd advise anyone to come. There's nothing to be frightened of.*"

"Gary"

"My migraines were so severe that I used to curl up in a ball crying with pain. I couldn't go into work. They would last for twelve hours and for up to six days. It didn't matter what pills I was swallowing. It got suicidal towards the end - it felt that there was nowhere else to go."

"I didn't know what to believe. I'd tried everything else and I had nothing to lose. Since healing, it's cut down from nineteen to twenty migraines per month to four to five. I don't lie on the floor crying with pain now. The migraines started at age seventeen and I've suffered for twenty-three years. During healing I get a hot sensation, which pulsates through to my eyes. There are shades of light pushing 'tingling' down to my feet."

"Diane"

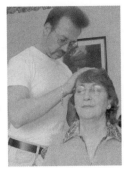

"*I found out that I had spondylosis of the spine, which caused quite severe problems for me not being able to walk. As a one parent mother with three children I knew that I really had to get my problems sorted. So I decided to go and see Andrew McKellar and he helped me greatly. It does take a long time to move that type of complaint but I can honestly say I do not have that disease now.*"

"*Following this I had a lump in my throat and they thought it was a tumour. I was due to go to the hospital but I told the consultant that I'd prefer to go to see Andrew McKellar and I had every confidence that this lump would disappear. I attended for three healing visits and, after the third visit, it took about another two weeks. One day the lump had completely disappeared.*"

"*Another time, because I'm very accident prone, I tripped over and I had a frozen ankle. Being in Andy's company one evening, he asked me what was wrong and I told him. He said, for goodness sake, you should have told me, I would have been able to help you again. I said – well as a friend I didn't really like to ask him another favour. However, he insisted and by twenty minutes I walked around the room like nothing was wrong with my foot. I have had no problems since.*"

"*When Andrew's giving me the healing I experience enormous heat. And this goes through my body and usually starts around the top of my head, gradually flowing through as he continues through my body. The other thing I see is beautiful lights – lovely emeralds and blues – mauves – just amazing formations like you would see in a rainbow. And a feeling of great calm afterwards – this helps me most. At the end of each session I feel so peaceful and calm when I walk away and I just think that everyone should experience this – not just a few.*"

"Giselle"

"I fell pregnant with my second baby and just out of the blue I got psoriasis all over. It was terrible. Before I had psoriasis I had perfect skin. Everyone used to tell me how nice it was. I went to my doctor and he said it was incurable. I wasn't happy with that so he sent me to a dermatologist at the hospital. He examined me and he said it was so bad he had only seen it in a textbook before. He said I would need to live with it because there was no cure. I went to another dermatologist and he told me the same thing. He told me it would never go away. I felt close to suicide."

"I then heard about you. From the first session it started going away and it's completely gone. Your hands felt very hot and I was always completely relaxed. If you hadn't been able to cure me I wouldn't be here today. I feel confident and I know that if I ever get psoriasis again, the only person I will contact is you."

"Heather"

"I was diagnosed at twenty-eight with asthma. As I got older it got worse. I couldn't walk anywhere. I did, but with great difficulty. I had to use an inhaler to get through the day and a medication mask over my mouth for ten minutes. The inhalers are steroids. Since my first visit they've been packed away. I don't go to the doctor anymore. Now I'm uphill and downhill! I'm fighting fit."

"Sharon"

"My mother came to see Andrew with shoulder problems. It was arthritis. By her third visit she could manage to do her own hair and she was very surprised. I was sceptical. We've all grown up to believe in nothing. However, I had endometriosis. It grows in the womb but also in the bowel and kidneys and spine. Most of my bowel was infected."

"The first time I came to Andrew I came with my mother. I was in a lot of pain and it was ruling my life. But once I stepped in the door I felt complete calm and a sense of peace. And really I thought I had to have an open mind that it was going to work."

"I felt intense heat - first on my back and then my stomach. Then it seemed to travel all over my body. There were beautiful colours - swirling. I had a sense of a magnet – being swayed – flying, virtually in mid air. By the third visit I wasn't taking any painkillers. I was able to sleep."

"The day I was admitted to hospital for surgery for the infected bowel, they came to me a few minutes before. They said don't be surprised if you wake up with a colostomy because the problem I'd got was very severe. I was very frightened but I thought of Andrew. They said I'd be in surgery for five hours. Well I was only in surgery for an hour. Most of the problem was gone. The bowel is fine now. They were really surprised at the hospital."

"Sheila"

"For the last twenty-five years I've suffered from asthma, which can be quite debilitating for everyday life. Just going up and down stairs, walking from a warm room to a cold room or from a cold room to a warm room, any form of exercise like walking the dog/ shopping/just really moving around or doing your housework. It can all affect your breathing. You become out of breath and you can't exhale. You start coughing and have to use your inhalers and sometimes I would also have to go in with a reliever - if I did any extra walking or shopping or up and down stairs - I would have to use it as well."

"Now I don't need any of them! I don't use them. I walk my dog, do housework and I just don't have a problem any more. When I came to see Andrew I was open-minded. I didn't really have any expectations and I was quite surprised actually - my asthma went almost instantly."

CHAPTER SIX

CHAPTER SIX

NEW HORIZONS

"Nobody trips over mountains. It is the small pebble that causes you to stumble.

Pass all the pebbles in your path and you will find you have crossed the mountain"

One of the most fascinating aspects of Andrew's team of spiritual colleagues from beyond is that no matter where he is, so are they. For someone who spent his formative years on the receiving end of so many "out-of-body" travelling experiences, it comes as quite a shock to learn that all through childhood, his teens, his troubled years in the wilderness and his starting out in employment, Andrew had never even been out of the United Kingdom.

Anyone else in his position probably would have "dipped the toe" in the travel department with a cheap package deal to the Costa Brava, or at the very least, a day trip to France. But, when Andrew did decide to get on a plane, he chose much bigger territories. Firstly, India, to enable him to experience Sai Baba's Ashram – an amazing journey both physically and mentally, and one he has been thrilled to repeat twice subsequently. And, secondly, the United States of America.

INDIA

The first time Andrew bit the bullet and set off for India in search of Sai Baba, he recalls fondly that the journey to reach the spiritual leader's birthplace – Puttaparthi in Southern India – was refreshingly straightforward. His second visit there a few years later was much the same. One flew into Bombay and then caught a plane to Bangalore. In keeping with his astral experiences, Andrew is clearly "up" for flying, never one willingly to waste precious time travelling the arduous way. Admittedly, in those days, what then greeted him as a place to stay was spartan and makeshift in the extreme, so the more comfortable the journey there and back, the more enjoyable the actual time spent there. Puttaparthi was a once tiny Indian village, literally now besieged by devotees. As far as Andrew was concerned, the two trips to India were enough. He felt absolutely no reason to repeat the experience. After all, Sai Baba "visited" him. So, why go again?

Or so he thought. Until in 1999 his wife Gerri had a profound dream. Sai Baba, she told Andrew, had told her in the dream that they must both go to India. He also said they should bring a group with them. Andrew was pretty frustrated. He really didn't believe it was a "call" for him to go. He confided in his wife that the only way he would change his mind would be if the guru came to him personally.

Which, of course, he duly did. Holding up two fingers in Andrew's dream, Sai Baba smiled and said "*Two tickets*." This was not going to go away.

Bridegroom Andrew with Best Man Mick Ingram

Newlyweds Andrew & Gerri

Andrew with Bride Gerri, Mick Ingram and "Jock" McKellar

Andrew in Buddy Holly wedding singer mode

Hint finally taken, Andrew and Gerri gathered together their chosen group of people, including Andrew's brother Kenny. And then, for a reason Andrew has yet to fathom out, they booked this dream-inspired third trip for Andrew, opting for a flight to Bombay and an onward train trip to Puttaparthi. An eighteen-hour train trip to Puttaparthi. It is this sort of story, related po-faced by Andrew, that reveals his wonderful sense of humour and ability to laugh at the worst that life can deliver.

This overland trip in the first class carriages of what sounds like a typical colonial train might have brought with it the very best of luxury, romance and history. A chance to experience unspoiled gems of yesteryear. A fitting mode of transport to complement a spiritual pilgrimage.

Or not.

"No – there wasn't anything remotely charming about it. In fact, I would rather travel on a bed of nails on the back of a donkey. We had sleeping quarters, but with four to a cabin, no air-conditioning, a variety of locals with a tendency to pass wind and a constant drone of snoring, it was a complete nightmare. And, to add insult to injury, Gerri had Delhi belly."

What greeted them though was, in Andrew's words, "*as close to a Garden of Eden as one can get.*" Time, and the efforts of the Sai Baba organisation, had transformed their destination into a completely blissful and unbelievably magnetic and energising haven. An Ashram the size of Southampton.

Their stay was a tremendous success for the group. So much so, Andrew's brother Kenny stayed on in India for six months. So, what does Andrew think the purpose of the trip actually was, I ask him, aside from discovering a phobia for train journeys. He replies that he hasn't a clue.

"*What you receive from Sai Baba is exactly what you need, not what you ask for.*"

UNITED STATES OF AMERICA

It's a wonder that Andrew ever risked going to bed. As often seems the case, horizontal on a mattress is his magnet for attracting disembodied voices. And often the invisible mouths deliver perplexing information. It was certainly the case one evening during Andrew's relationship with Rose. As if from nowhere, whilst he was settling down in bed one evening, the voice piped up:

"*Andrew – go to America.*"

And, almost as if the voice had anticipated that the message was unwelcome, it persevered with those four words some three more times in all.

Andrew confesses that the statement grated. America was, at the time, not on his "wish list" and the mere idea of having to organise himself to go to such a huge continent, when he had already established a demanding healing service in the UK, was bothersome in the extreme.

But then came a telephone call a couple of days later from some friends in Winter Haven, Florida. America was not going away. Peeved or not, Andrew and Rose were suddenly across the Pond, Disney-bound, staying with their friends Gill and Graham and being introduced to the Reverend Bill Achor, a minister for the Science of Spirituality organisation.

The voice at least had the decency not to crow "I told you so."

Andrew offered to give the Reverend some healing for troublesome neck and knee problems. So smitten was Bill Achor with the healing results, he asked Andrew if he might consider giving a talk to a few people during his stay in the States and Andrew was delighted to oblige.

All eighty-something of them.

The venue for the talk was the Reverend Achor and his wife Diane's personal home sitting room. To Andrew McKellar from Southampton, England this meant a small parlour gathering. But he hadn't bargained on the sheer scale of the room. Word had got around. Andrew was in town and the town was turning out in force, squeezing enthusiastically into the Achors' larger-than-life living space and hanging on to Andrew's every word.

Not surprisingly, Andrew and Rose's holiday had suddenly been hijacked. The following day Andrew was swamped with locals with pleas for healing. He casts his mind back to a particularly touching case – a couple with an eight month old baby arrived, at their wits end trying to cope with their child's terrible stomach condition. The baby had so many tumours in the stomach area that a normal nappy was out of the question. The parents had had to resort to a large towel with a safety pin. Andrew held the child close, placed his hands on the stomach and astounded those gathered with the complete silence of the baby. Within a couple of days, the baby was able to wear a normal nappy and the couple's specialist admitted to being dumbfounded.

Andrew's visit to America was a fabulous experience and he would certainly never again begrudge a nagging voice telling him to return. Andrew's Winter Haven patients were in awe of his gift and, in turn, he was bowled over by the unconditional support that greeted him from the moment he stepped off the plane. His second visit saw him ordained as a Science of Spirituality minister himself – a tremendous honour in recognition of his healing gift and contribution made during that first visit.

To date Andrew has four US trips under his belt, each one illustrating just how welcoming and open-minded American townsfolk can be. In fact, he describes some of his support there as reminiscent of Beatlemania. Gerri and he have literally had to barricade themselves in to suites they have hired for public healing sessions because enthusiasm has been so exuberant. Americans, Andrew has discovered, faced with inexplicable healing evidence, embrace rather than crush; explore rather than stand still and encourage others to experience rather than dismissing as impossible.

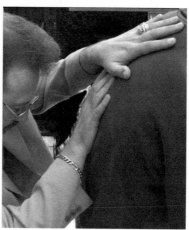

Always working

I watch a video of Andrew's American healing experiences. Dr John O'Neill is an alternative medicine practitioner in the States and Director of the Clearwater Natural Medical Centre. An acupuncture physician, he runs a centre, which also provides homeopathic, herbal, vitamin and mineral health treatments. He was first introduced to Andrew several years ago by one of his patients and is clearly one of Andrew's greatest supporters:

"I am very deeply impressed with Andrew McKellar – his healing abilities, his integrity, his entire being as a person. He has worked on many of my patients, with outstanding results. When you're worked on by Andrew it's not something abstract. Spiritual Healing sometimes sounds abstract. It's something that everyone, sceptics included, can feel. You can feel the heat of his hands. You can feel sensations moving through your body, and afterwards too. It's not something you have to take on faith. It's something you can directly experience and, when you see person after person, who have been stumbling, on crutches and wracked with pain, suddenly, spontaneously, dramatically recover, it's really awe-inspiring, deeply humbling and ultimately challenges us to think about what healing really is. As a health professional I think it's our duty to wake up every morning trying to figure out how to put ourselves out of work - namely to heal people. And this is one of the most profound ways."

Andrew, ever succinct, simply gives me a short resume of his American experiences. On watching some of his USA video clips however, I discover wonderful testimonies from American patients he has healed. The most heart-warming and impressive excerpt is that of Michelle. Hers is a horror story. We see her arriving in a wheelchair for her session with Andrew. She is a young woman, who has learned to live with extreme discomfort – migraines, freezing and numb extremities, constant pain. She is clearly used to continual discomfort and lack of energy. Watching her "Before and After" interview footage is a joy:

"MICHELLE"

"When I came in my feet were numb and cold. I had a migraine. My neck was very stiff. I've had a very serious back injury with a lot of scar tissue – disc damage, torn discs. Very painful. I've been in bed for a long time so my muscles are all shot – atrophied. As soon as Andrew started work on me I could feel intense heat. The spasms settled down immediately, which also settled the pain down rather immediately as well. As soon as he put his hands on my head I felt tingling. It felt really hot and when he took them away the tingling lingered. The migraine's gone – my neck has loosened up – my vision is more clear. He worked down my legs and up and down my spine. The heat is still there. It's been over half an hour now and the heat is still with me. The pain relief is still with me. The spasming [sic] hasn't come back. My legs feel light and tingling – peculiar – but they don't hurt. And my feet are warm for the first time in weeks. My feet have been stone cold. I've had them under two big thick blankets and a quilt at home, two pairs of socks and a pair of hand-knitted slippers. And still they were turning blue. I have suffered with the spinal problem for over ten years."

~~~

Andrew's video of his American trip features healing sessions with many other patients. Had I not watched it through, I would have had no real inkling of his popularity there, nor the tremendous admiration held for him by Dr O'Neill. Andrew was content just to say a few, modest words:

"I travelled to America. Well, in fact I was "called" to Florida – a place called Winter Haven. I was told by voices to go. We had some friends there and they introduced me to friends needing healing. Inevitably the planned holiday trip turned into a two week working vacation. I loved the States because they were so much more positive. The British tend to be spiritually backward in accepting what's possible. In the States they are so open to this sort of work – even doctors. I worked with Doctor John O'Neill there. I would love to do more in America and I know I'll go back there."

And, beyond a shadow of a doubt, you too just "know" that he will.

SCEPTICS

The medical profession will scoff.
The medical profession will whinge.
The medical profession will laugh.
The medical profession will cringe.

They say that healing is nonsense,
but what do they really know
about the power of healing -
the power that freely flows.

In their ignorance of darkened, closed minds
they slander and mock - try to scare.
I smile to myself as I watch them.
I smile as they pull out their hair.

What foolish people to say
they are on a mission of love
to fight that greater force -
the power of unconditional love.

Yes, this power does more than they say
in infinite ways every day.
In time foolish sceptics shall see
Spiritual Healing works.
Eternally.

24 March 2003
Andrew McKellar

"Simply Divine"

Down through the ages we have been taught that God is something "outside" ourselves. In many religious practices, people have had encrusted into their minds that God is something to fear.

The time has come when people are awakening. After centuries of ignorance and fear, people are awakening to Spirituality; awakening to the reality that everything that breathes, everything that lives, is God. So, yes, you yourself are God. You are divine by nature. God resides within your very being.

Our responsibility is to realise this, to nurture, to know God within.

We must learn to forgive others, even those who do wrong to us. We must cultivate love and compassion for all forms of life. Love is the key to awakening the God within. Not selfish love, by loving that which you *want* to love.

Once you awaken to the divine within, you shall awaken to the divine in others, thereby seeing life in a different light. Your state of consciousness rises to a higher level. Thereafter you slowly become cleansed in spirit, mind and body.

Once man awakens to this truth, the dark pits of illness and disease shall be filled with love and harmony. By banishing the bate of illness, negative force cannot take hold. Ignorance, jealousy, envy, revenge, hate, desire for selfishness, greed and other forms of negative mind activity slowly dissolve in the water of love and knowledge.

You are divine. Realise this truth. If you say this baby girl is mother, people would not understand. The baby girl shall grow into a woman and one day become a mother. Grow in the knowledge that you are divine and, as you grow, you shall realise divine qualities.

And, finally, the child of ignorance shall be the Mother of Knowledge:

God aware.
God knowing,
God realised.

Received in a meditative state
By Andrew McKellar

CHAPTER SEVEN

ENDINGS, BEGINNINGS AND DREAMS

**"There is a wonderful law of nature
that the three things we crave most
- happiness, freedom and peace of mind -
are always attained by giving them to someone else"**

Finally, Andrew's relationship with Rose came to an end. She had been several years older than him and, whilst they had shared considerable time together and experienced much of Andrew's developing progress as a couple, Andrew decided to break off the relationship.

It was time to move home, yet again, in Southampton – to a house in Shirley. Packing his clothes and belongings into suitcases and a variety of black sacks, Andrew became irritated that he couldn't lay his hands on a book he was particularly keen on. "Phonecalls from the Dead" was a favourite read for him and frustratingly absent, just when he needed to find it. He couldn't remember when he'd last seen it but clearly it was well camouflaged for the moment and stubbornly evading Andrew's attempts to locate it. Finally, he admitted defeat and went to retrieve the last of his black bags to go. And there it was, squarely positioned on the floor in the middle of the bedroom doorway. Phonecalls from the Dead - clearly game for a laugh. And Andrew moved on.

As did his love life. In 1997 he was approached by a woman asking him to give a talk at her house. He had met Gerri, his future wife.

"We started to have spiritual experiences indicating that we had been together in previous lives. Gerri already had a daughter – Kristie-Anne. We all rented a house from a patient. A year later we married and had a child together – Marcus, now five. Gerri is a very gifted medium in her

*own right. By this time healing was my career and my life. I was treating
all ailments. Gerri told me about two to three years ago – you will treat a
lot of cancer patients."*

With their new lives together, Andrew and Gerri would stay up late, often
chatting in the kitchen, generally getting to know each other better, as
new couples do. It was during such a chat one evening that Andrew noticed
a tiny ball of light suddenly appear in the kitchen doorway. Gerri had her
back to the door, so that Andrew found himself half listening to what she
was saying and distractedly keeping an eye on the moving sphere too. It
moved up to the ceiling and suddenly Gerri was looking up. She'd spotted
it too. They both watched it disperse. Then just as suddenly, they both
became aware of a presence. An old lady, short with white hair and a
white, thick-knitted shawl had joined them in the room. She was bent
over and only able to move with a stick. Fascinated, they watched her
until then she just faded away.

It was a few weeks later than an elderly gentleman in his eighties came to
Andrew for healing for arthritis in his hips. *"Changed in here hasn't it?"*
he said. *"It was lot different when I used to live here."*

Andrew and Gerri were living in the very house this new patient had been
born in. Andrew asked if he remembered an old lady with a white shawl
and difficulty getting around. *"Oh yes"*, he said. *"That would be Beatrice.
She lived next door. She was always stood at the gate!"*

Gerri and Andrew decided it was the right time to buy a home of their
own. When the house opposite went on the market Andrew approached
the owner to buy it, somewhat wrong footing him by confirming that he
had no need to "view" the property. He had, in fact, already had a dream
that he would purchase it. He had "seen" the rear garden area of the
property in precise detail, even though he had never stepped foot in it, nor
ever received any description of it from anyone. And, when he and the
vendor stood in the garden together, it was exactly as Andrew had seen it.
The deal was done.

Andrew had "seen" everything to do with the house. Except the invisible children. In the familiar spiritual "gallery" of the bedroom, Andrew and Gerri were both about to experience a soundtrack without the film. It was about two o'clock in the morning one night when Gerri shook Andrew awake. *"Can you hear that? Someone's opened the front door."* So Andrew went into 'it-must-be-burglar' mode again and gamely went downstairs to check. He found nothing wrong.

One hour later Gerri was disturbing him again: *"Someone's running up the stairs – two girls – teenagers."* Once again a search revealed nothing.

And then one morning, around dawn, Andrew himself awoke to the sound of the front door opening and slamming shut. Immediately he heard the thud, thud, thud of feet on the stairs and the sound of breathless laughter you hear when children are chasing each other in fun. To Andrew, it sounded like two young teenage girls. What's more, they were now running along the passageway heading for Andrew and Gerri's bedroom. Sitting bolt upright in bed and watching Gerri sleeping on peacefully, he had no option but to listen to the girls tumble into the bedroom and proceed to taunt each other, one each side of the bed. And then, one ran back out of the room, taking the other with her hot on her heels; they thudded back down the stairs and exited noisily out of the front door. It was as if Andrew and Gerri simply didn't exist.

For no other reason than they needed to plan for more space for Andrew's healing, there followed yet another move about a year later when they bought a four-bedroom house in Southampton's Millbrook area. This time there was an annexe for healing. This was their first "sanctuary" and, in Andrew's words, absolutely beautiful.

Of course, such is the way of life, just as things were going so well, Andrew received news from his father that his health was going downhill. Against Andrew's advice, Malcolm McKellar had continued to smoke. The result was that he needed an urgent heart bypass. Andrew, Gerri and their little boy Marcus travelled up to see him and they were shocked that he seemed to feel that he didn't have long to live. They returned home to Southampton and the night before the bypass was due to take place, Andrew received a call from his father. He was ringing to say goodbye. He was utterly convinced that he wouldn't survive the operation.

However, contrary to his suspicions, the operation went extremely well and after just two days he was out of intensive care. Andrew made sure that he was on the spot to give him as much healing as possible and, during the first week of recuperation, the doctor remarked on how well the major surgical scar had healed. He commented to Andrew that it had taken on the appearance one would expect to see in a scar two years old – not a handful of days old.

Sadly, Andrew's father's condition suddenly worsened. He had another stroke – this time massive. Time was clearly running out and the family was called together to spend what little time was left, gathered around the hospital bed. This was a tense and sad time and perhaps not the best moment for Andrew's wife Gerri to start going into a trance state. As mentioned previously, Gerri is a talented spiritual medium in her own right but this was probably not an appropriate venue to start communicating with the dead.

However, try as she might to stay grounded, a very persistent Scottish voice was not going away. It belonged to a tiny woman with, as Gerri put it, "masses of black hair". The message, repeated time and again, was the same:

"Ma name's Annie and I've come for ma laddie."

As is often the nature of messages received from "the other side", no one, absolutely no one within the gathered family, could shed any light on who an "Annie" might have been. It was a complete mystery. However, the McKellar Family also boasted a far from conventional history. Andrew's father had had two sisters – Betty and Helen. Their parents had parted when they were all young. Their mother had remained in the UK with Andrew's father, who never spoke about his mother when Andrew was growing up. But their father had taken both sisters to America. Andrew's father finally met his two sisters again only three years prior to his own death.

So, Andrew returned home and telephoned his American aunts. He needed to let them know that his father was sadly not going to recover. And he asked them whether or not the name "Annie" rang a bell with them – a lady who was noticeably tiny and with an equally noticeable shock of dark hair. The sisters were almost dumbstruck. *"Oh my God, Andrew. We can stop searching now. Our mother's name was Annie Brown. She was less than five feet tall and renowned for her thick, dark hair. We've been trying to trace her. Now we shan't have to worry any more."*

It was an uplifting moment in an otherwise utterly miserable period. The following day, Andrew's father passed away. Ironically, he had succumbed to the much-feared hospital superbug, MRSA. Andrew would miss his hard-headed Scots father. But he was comforted to know that Malcolm McKellar had finally been reunited with his mother Annie.

Life would clearly never be quite the same for Andrew. Thankfully, he had made fantastic progress with his healing and had developed a reputation for being able to help the full range of medical conditions. He needed to remain focused on his healing path. Demand was increasing and the more people he healed, the more enquiries he received. However, with people for treatment, come practical issues. Like parking. After eighteen months they simply needed more room for patient parking space. Andrew knew someone in a village called Burridge – a new part of the Southampton area for him, with a real countryside feel to it still.

'Dream' House, – new home, new sanctuary, new neighbours...

"*A house came to Gerri in a dream. It had a half-moon-shaped, gravel driveway and she felt that it had an American-style "chalet bungalow" appearance about it, with the garage very definitely on the right-hand side of the property.*"

And of course, they quickly discovered that just such a house was on the market. Another deal was done. Burridge was to become their new home, a lovely place for their children to be, an ideal place for Andrew's new Healing Sanctuary.

And a complete and utter nightmare.

"MARCUS"

It would be quite early in their relationship that Gerri would accompany Andrew on a trip to Newport Richey in Florida. Andrew knew this stay in the States would be more healing than leisure. In advance of their arrival, one of Andrew's friends in Florida had put the word out that Andrew McKellar, healer would be arriving. There was much work to be done.

Demand for Andrew was, as usual, phenomenal. He would collapse into bed shattered each night. Gerri and Andrew had no plans at the time to have more children. But Gerri announced to Andrew one morning that she had had a profound experience the night before, which she couldn't explain. She had seen a spirit form come towards her from their bedroom wall. The lady in question was carrying a baby in her arms and holding the child out towards Gerri.

Back in England shortly afterwards, Gerri discovered she was pregnant. She had another spirit visitation. This time it was from her own spirit guide "Lanto", who told her that the baby should be treasured "*because he was once a lama from Tibet – a holy being*".

Yeh, sure, thought Andrew.

But a few weeks later Andrew had a sudden out-of-body experience again. He was aware that there were doctors looking over a couch and Andrew somehow "knew" that there was a baby on the couch. He watched as one of the male doctors lifted the baby up and walked over to him, placing it in his arms. Andrew was struck at how long the baby was and his attention was also drawn to a rather distinctive mark just above the baby's top lip.

"*This child is coming to you*", said the doctor. "*Look after him. He was a lama. He will do much good in the world.*"

And so Marcus was born. And, strangely enough, Marcus was an extremely long baby with a mark above his top lip at birth. But, stranger still was the response Andrew received from an Indian acquaintance he knew – a former interpreter of the Tibetan Dalai Lama himself. When showed a photograph of baby Marcus all he would repeat enthusiastically was "lama, lama, lama!"

And, strangest of all, when Marcus uttered his first words, they weren't the normal baby words for mummy or daddy that one might expect.

No, Marcus's first words were "swami, swami", spoken whilst pointing to a picture of Andrew's guru Sai Baba. "Swami" is a term commonly used in India to address or refer to a guru. It is not a term ever used by Andrew or Gerri.

But it was by Marcus. In Southampton. Aged two.

"BABY"

A few years ago I heard my spiritual teacher Sai Baba telepathically say to me:

"Once the baby leaves the darkness of the womb it shall recognise its mother. The baby, while in the womb is dark, encompassed in protection. Once brought into the light of day there is an instant recognition with mother. The baby does not fully understand or fully know the mother. But the instant recognition causes the baby to trust implicitly.

So, when man awakens from his long sleep and frees himself from the dark womb of constant material thought, he shall grow, develop and learn much about himself. And, like the baby, shall receive the mother's full attention, and love, protection and guidance."

"Yes, once man awakens to spiritual truth, his true mother of life shall guide him to the kingdom of love and light."

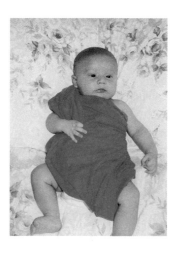

Marcus – Ex Lama – dressing the part already!

CHAPTER EIGHT

CHAPTER EIGHT

GOOD PRESS, BAD NEWS

**"Do not follow where the path may lead.
Go instead where there is no path and leave a trail"**

Happily installed in their new, detached Burridge home and with their new Nirvana Healing Sanctuary perfectly positioned, Andrew and Gerri were now looking forward to wonderful things. Their dreams of finding the right place to combine home, family and working life had been realised. Press articles in the Hampshire region about Andrew's healing powers and miracle success stories were by now not uncommon.

It was ironic then that the glowing praise for Andrew's unique gift, featured by a patient in her local health and beauty publication, should fuel the start of a vitriolic and very public battle. The patient in question had been suffering with a torn ligament in her right foot, coupled with severe tendonitis for almost a year. Karen Ralls had arrived a total sceptic at Andrew's house. However, following a series of healing sessions, she was completely cured, free from crutches, released from pain and able to return to driving. What should have been superb publicity and a huge tribute to Andrew appears to have opened the door for neighbours in his new road to launch a tough campaign to stop Andrew working from his home.

"Within a matter of a couple of days next door was complaining about cars arriving in the drive. We were entering almost two years of trouble. We've had verbal abuse and property damage. Someone tried to throw a brick through our front window and scattered tacks in my driveway. We've received countless anonymous letters through the door."

Karen's article had been headed up *"World famous healer moves to Burridge"* and had detailed her original scepticism together with her subsequent delight. Andrew's photograph was included as well. Later in her feature she went on to say *"He is indeed a tremendous asset to the people of Burridge."*

A couple of days after moving into his new house, one of Andrew's next door neighbours was passing as Andrew was getting out of his car. *"A privilege to have you in the street is it. We'll see about that won't we"*, he told Andrew.

Almost immediately the local council began to receive a number of complaints from neighbours. Residents complained about the Healing Sanctuary welcoming patients out of normal office hours; they took exception in particular to the increase in the number of cars visiting the house. The vehicles, they claimed, were causing noise disturbance, such as doors slamming and setting off car alarms. Then there were the cracks in the road …

Shortly afterwards a letter arrived from the borough council ordering Andrew to cease business. He contacted the council but they warned him that if he did continue with his healing sanctuary, they would send an enforcement notice. *"I see my healing as a service to mankind. Why should I allow them to shut me down."* Andrew says.

He pointed out to the official that he had patients relying on him and that closing the sanctuary down would inevitably get into the press and, possibly, on to the TV. He didn't want to be egotistical but why should he let people down? The council official's response was negative:

"They won't be able to do anything."

That was enough for Andrew. Now he really was angry. He decided to apply for full planning permission. Meanwhile, two neighbours in particular were continuing to distribute warnings about Andrew's presence in the road. Their claims were becoming more serious. They maintained that Andrew's business would completely swamp the road with cars. Children could be killed by Andrew McKellar's patients' cars. Andrew's integrity itself was put under scrutiny with references to his owning a

Mercedes and his wife driving a four-wheel drive, when the healing business operated on "donations". Wildlife would be threatened. The list of complaints grew, as did the number of objectors. Andrew could simply do no right.

In order to see what residents were writing about him, Andrew had even purchased the letters. None of these objectors actually knew Andrew well. In his view they were simply on a mission to scaremonger.

The wording of the letter he remembers best is etched in his memory. It contained sentences like:

"Before Mr McKellar moved into Burridge Road, you could clearly hear the tentative step of the doe looking for its young as it slowly trotted along; you could also hear the whoosh of the winged owl flying low and the insects crawling across the road looking for their grubs."

The gloves were clearly off.

As was the poetic prose.

At the council meeting to agree a way forward for the residents, Andrew won his case but it was decreed that he could only see restricted numbers of patients, with restricted working hours. This puzzled Andrew because there were other businesses in Burridge Road free of such restrictions. So he appealed and took his complaint to the Secretary of State. Their representative felt that the driveway was suitable for the expected volume of cars. He ruled that Andrew could see slightly more patient numbers and work between the hours of nine and five Monday to Friday.

Ultimately, the complaints had started with just two neighbours and had then risen to over twenty. Andrew and his family became paranoid about setting foot outside their home. However, an article in the Southampton Echo newspaper featuring Andrew's plight went some way to tipping the balance of opinion. Then a television documentary 'Inside Out' featured testimonies from patients whom Andrew had cured of cancer, together with the TV presenter Chris Packham's mother receiving healing over a period of a month herself. She had been happy to go on camera full of praise at the end of the programme. It helped to turn the tide of opinion once and for all. Neighbour complaints reduced from twenty-two to eight. Suddenly, Andrew was receiving support from fellow residents. Some said they were appalled at how he had been treated. They agreed that objectors referring to the road as a 'cul-de-sac' were deliberately misrepresenting the sheer size of the road. It is, in fact, wide and fairly long, with houses placed well back from the actual road. Suddenly, Andrew was hearing comments not dissimilar to those made in the original press article:

"It's a privilege to have you here."

Andrew, it would seem, was once again 'PC'.

Even the neighbour directly opposite Andrew and Gerri gave them his support. Andrew had taken his case to the highest possible authority to enable him to work with his patients Monday to Friday. And he had won. Had he not, there would have been no choice but to turn away a considerable number of new patients, adding more to the waiting list and running the risk of not being able to see them until it was, potentially, too late to help.

I am prompted to ask Andrew a series of questions, lingering at the back of my mind all the while I have been listening to this tale of woe and hopes dashed.

– *Why do you think, spiritually, you've been given these problems?*
– *All you want to do is help people with health problems. So why is it proving such an uphill struggle? Do some people see you as a crank?*
– *Do you think there's something you need to learn?*

Andrew's reply, given the sheer frustration and lengthy period of uncertainty he and his family have endured, is remarkably philosophical and lacking in resentment. Not surprisingly, it is based around a Sai Baba quotation taken from an old French saying:

"Anyone 'unusual' is like a tree bearing fruit; always, it always get sticks thrown at it."

Behind him a bitter experience. But not a bitter man.

The move to Burridge should also have been an opportunity for Andrew to put his father's death behind him. But he did miss him tremendously and never a day went by without his "asking" his father to speak to him, to visit, to show himself. Gerri had seen her late father-in-law on more than one occasion. Andrew found this comforting but still rather unfulfilling.

And then, as suddenly as they always came, Andrew had two highly significant out-of-body experiences. The first saw him one evening in bed, suddenly out of his body and into a tunnel of stunning white light. There, coming from behind a large white building – rather like an opera house – was his father, as large as life. He said to Andrew: *"Death - it's not what you think – you can't die."* And with that, Andrew found himself straight back in his body and in bed. He remembers his father looked free of anxiety, released from pain and totally without fear. It had been the briefest of meetings but it meant the world to Andrew.

It left him feeling much happier until, a few months later, he had a similar experience, this time finding himself sitting on a rock by a stream, with his father suddenly talking to him from his side. On this occasion, however, their meeting would leave Andrew with a sensation of dread. His father had had a worried look on his face – *"as if he wanted to tell me something.*

His eyes were welling up. I kissed him on the cheek."

Andrew received no message at all from his father but he knew, beyond a shadow of a doubt, that his father had wanted to warn him of something around the corner; something that Andrew would find very tough to accept.

Something was wrong with his mother.

Andrew and mum... getting closer!

Andrew lodged a call to his mother at the earliest opportunity, desperately trying to make chit-chat whilst all the while needing to ask her if she felt all right. Hardly an easy task. As far as he could tell, all was well.

But then, not long afterwards, came the unwelcome news. Yes, something was indeed wrong. A check-up at the local hospital had revealed a problem. Andrew's mother had cancer of the oesophagus. Andrew had known that the news would inevitably come. He trusted his meeting with his father. So, saddened and hugely disappointed for his mother, Andrew did the only thing he knew how. He began healing for her.

Chemotherapy was suggested by his mother's consultant. She declined. She needed a strong immune system and, ultimately, Andrew believes she knew she was dying. However, she agreed to an operation to remove the tumour. This was major surgery and it revealed that she also had a tumour in the stomach. The specialist spoke with Andrew about the findings from the surgical procedure. He had been surprised to note that the tumour in his mother's stomach had been dead. He was also astounded at how quickly Mrs McKellar had made her recovery after the operation. Literally, only two days after leaving hospital she was out shopping in Southampton.

But Andrew's mother, just like his father, was a committed smoker and all through her illness continued to smoke forty cigarettes a day. The cancer went into her lungs and Andrew continued to administer healing to help ease her symptoms, all the while knowing that her time was probably about to come. And it did. In June 2001 Andrew's mother passed away. And Andrew was devastated.

He felt sure that his mother would contact him. Every night following her death he would ask her to come. And every night she simply didn't show up. Not a sign, not a voice. Nothing.

Not one to be proved wrong, Andrew persevered with his daily request and then, quite dramatically about a year later, bingo. He had another, totally unexpected out-of-body experience, finding himself standing right in front of his mother, as if she were as alive and fit as ever. She spoke to her son very firmly and left him in no doubt as to her situation:

"Don't worry about me – I'm all right. Andrew I'm fine."

From the moment he returned from the experience, he stopped grieving. He had now lost both his parents, people he had only really got to know properly at a late age, when so many years had been lost. And now they were gone. And so was their illness and suffering. So that was OK. Because there is no such thing as death.

So why be sad?

"BLUEY"

Ever have any luck treating pets? I ask during one of our sessions with house brick. Stupid question. By Andrew's expression I realise we could be in for a veritable zoo of four-legged, feathery success stories. On reflection though, not such a dumb question because these are "patients", who can't testify can they. Andrew will have to be spokesperson for them. He stresses that, much as he adores animals, he has been forced to limit healing because he has to give human patients priority. There is that patient waiting list and there is, after all, only one of Andrew. However, help animals from time to time, he certainly has.

Take Coco the New Forest horse, whose legs stopped functioning. A whisker's breadth away from being put down by the vet. Post-healing, Coco was cantering around a field, giving fellow companions a run for their money.

Then there was Amber the whippet, struck down with countless tumours and, according to her vet, not long for this world. A few healing sessions on, Amber's tumours had vanished.

He recalls friends Les and Eileen, upset that their cat had probably been hit by a vehicle. Like Toffee the calf, the cat was a law unto itself and Andrew was warned to touch at his peril. But his "hands-on" failed to generate even one claw in response and, by the time Andrew was in his car, the cat and two owners were all by the window to watch his departure.

And, on a visit with Gerri to an elderly friend near Glastonbury, Andrew tells how he watched their hostess's cat proudly enter the sitting room, dead trophy in mouth. The poor bird had blood coming from its beak and was lifeless. Andrew cupped it in his hands for several minutes and it suddenly sat up in the palm of his hand and took off for freedom.

Well, some animals do have a capacity for "playing dead" in the wild, I say. Perhaps that's what happened with the bird? Andrew is aware of the phenomenon but he is sure this wasn't one of those. His hands had been burning. He is certain that the bird was dead.

Sadly, Andrew isn't always able to help. Whilst with Rose, he was given a pet by a patient. Bluey was a colossus of a cat. An amber-eyed, Persian Blue with a motor of a purr to match his stature. Where Andrew went, Bluey followed. His faithful shadow. They made an inseparable team. He recalls picking him out of the litter and thinking *"This one's not going to be here long, so I must have him."* His hunch was to be proven correct. Whilst Andrew was in India, Bluey developed kidney problems. He was left with the vet while decisions were being reached. He was still only five. Back from India by now, Andrew awoke in bed to hear Bluey's unmistakable, resonant purr. But Bluey was still at the vet. Andrew knew his pet wouldn't make it. Shortly afterwards, the vet agreed to put Bluey to sleep at Andrew's home, rather than at the surgery. Andrew was inconsolable.

Years passed. Andrew never forgot his favourite cat. And then, one night when he was married to Gerri, he suddenly felt a presence in the room. Solid, surrounded by a glow of light and sitting up rabbit-like on his hind legs (a Bluey "trademark" trick from years before), sat Bluey. He proceeded to trot out of the door and had vanished by the time Andrew made it on to the landing. And, a few weeks later he returned. This time it was Gerri saying *"There's a Persian Blue cat here!"*, although she had no prior knowledge of Bluey.

Well she did now. Bluey in death was every inch the lion he had been in life.

R.I.P

"MATERIAL WEST"

In the tree there nests a nest; in the nest there are two eggs; in time the eggs shall break to reveal two chicks. The chicks will grow eventually leaving the nest. Being free from the restricted limitations, they fly to their freedom.

When man is born into the material world, he seeks not freedom; he seeks to build his nest – stronger, larger, higher – until his nest is so large it blacks out all light from entering within.

Received in a meditative state
By Andrew McKellar

CHAPTER NINE

CHAPTER NINE

BAG OF TOOLS AND COLOUR CHART

**"The one who says it cannot be done
should never interrupt the one who is doing it"**

It has now been several months of meeting with Andrew McKellar to discuss this biography. February 2003 seems an age ago in itself. Spring bulbs have come and gone and we now have British Summertime for heaven's sake. Our discussions, with faithful house brick, are a truly interesting and uplifting experience. But our get-togethers are, by necessity, an evening routine. Access to Andrew during a normal working day is devoted to those with health gremlins. Which, I am the first to concede, is quite right too.

Thus, our book sessions are nocturnal affairs and my morning-after tape transcription often hopelessly under-estimated, finding me superglued to keyboard way past rush hour. The cassette tape of each session often features Andrew stifling a series of yawns and apologising profusely for appearing rude. Rarely one to take offence, I realise that this is nothing personal. It serves as no bad reminder of how Andrew has to commit to his work. Sick people come to him every working day. And often they're sick people who aren't just a bit "off colour". These are people who are as sick as you can get. They're at the wrong end of months, sometimes years of pain; they've had to live through debilitating and crippling symptoms; far too often, they've been told by the medical profession that there really is absolutely no hope. These aren't people making hay; these are people making plans. To die.

So, by now I am beginning to grasp a bit better just how draining such patient activity must be for a healer. I thought I did understand but it's a bit like the glaringly obvious difference between a Brownie Box black and white photograph and a sophisticated computer software programme in glorious technicolour. Worlds, if not solar systems, apart.

Inevitably, I find myself increasingly curious as to how it all works – this healing business. And almost embarrassed to ask. I have trawled through a considerable number of patient testimonies. Young, old, male, female, smiles, tears, United Kingdom, America, wheelchairs, crutches, callipers, lumps, bumps and blotches. Andrew himself seems to have instant recollection of individual clients and their enormous range of medical problems. Often one story will trigger a recollection of a case history, still fresh in his mind and seemingly plucked from nowhere. The stories flow.

So, I am now at a stage where I am fit to burst with video interviews from over a decade, all confirming the facts behind his remarkable success stories. I have experienced enormous highs and even greater lows, sitting daily at my computer, reliving on his behalf a lifetime to date of wondrous experiences and perfectly awful events too. Trying to do it all justice, when one never has been, isn't currently and actually never will be a healer.

"The book is in the pen" apparently. But have I remembered to put the ink in? I find myself musing.

I am, I suspect, and with the greatest respect, somewhat guru'd out. What feels right now is to delve deeper into how Andrew McKellar actually does what he does. What feels right is to put down on paper Andrew's views on what really happens when he lays his hands on people. If I'm honest, what feels right now is to be unashamedly nosy.

Well, nobody's perfect.

"This healing gift isn't me, you know. The energy that comes through my hands to heal patient conditions is simply channelled <u>through</u> me from the higher source – I may be one of the chosen few but I'm still just the bag of tools."

I have finally steered Andrew McKellar on to the subject of how his healing methods actually operate and work. He recognises that it is a serious question for a naturally sceptical world and he wants to get his answer right. He very sweetly pauses for a moment and looks up to the ceiling politely to "ask" his helpers and guides to provide him with the instruction leaflet for the spiritual toolkit. And I will learn straight away that this is a handbook in full rainbow colour. In fact "steering" is probably no bad way to describe how I am encouraging Andrew to manoeuvre into a focused position to explain his healing. Because suddenly we're talking motor cars and fuel.

"Your car runs on petrol or diesel. If you fail to put either in, you struggle to carry on your journey. And, in the end, you run out altogether. Very few people know or realise that the body's energy system is fuelled by colour energy. At birth the colours are more or less in balance. Within the body you have several energy points – chakras – from the very base of the spine right up to the top of the head. Each energy point, in turn, has its own colour energy."

"When we're born, usually these colours are pretty much in balance. Then the exposure to stress begins – school, family, marriage, work, religion even – they can all cause pressures, which can then take root. They translate into weaknesses in the physical body. They lead to anxiety, discomfort and often pain. We lose colour energy. We get problems."

"And then, when we lose too much colour energy, we get big problems. And we get the medical profession saying there's very little or sometimes nothing else at all that they can do to help."

We pause to allow me to take in Andrew's words. And it strikes me that I've always assumed that somebody's being "off colour" is simply a description of the pallor, redness, yellowness, blueness even, that people outwardly display when they're not up to scratch physically. The "You look like I feel" inspiration when someone's hung over or going down with 'flu.

To Andrew McKellar "off colour" is far more to do with what's going on inside from birth; the hidden colour palette within, exposed to emotional pollution and deterioration, begging to be colour re-energised by a healer. He lists the locations of the colour energies he works with:

Base of spine	~	Red	Throat area	~	Blue
Just below navel	~	Orange	Heart region	~	Green
Solar plexus	~	Yellow	In between eyes	~	Indigo
		Very top of head	~	Violet	

He believes that each chakra reflects powerful emotional energies within our bodies. The heart region is, naturally enough, the emotional engine; the throat chakra the communication bridge. And so on. Allow the colour in one or more of those regions to fade, or badly distort, and you will land yourself with positive energy literally mutating into negative energy.

He describes what happens when a new patient comes to his healing room for their first session. Putting them at ease is a priority.

To begin, Andrew will greet his patient and, as he puts it, be at pains to ensure that there's *"No preaching. More likely or not I'll crack a joke or two."* They will then have a brief review of the medical problems to be overcome. They are sitting in a healing room that is calm, bright, functional and private – relatively free of spiritual references and definitely void of the tackier "spiritual paraphernalia", of which Andrew has a horror. Already, he will be observing the visitor's body without their even realising it.

Healing Sanctuary inspirational companion

"Green" is Andrew's great "getting started" tool. He explains that, more often than not, he will see a greenish mist wherever a problem lies. Ironically, it helps him if patients dress in lighter colours, purely because it's tougher for him to spot the mist if he's confronted with hues like blacks, browns or dark blues.

Green is his highly useful "pointer" but Andrew stresses that it only steers him to the correct problem areas. It doesn't diagnose the exact nature of the condition.

It will now be time for Andrew to attune to the higher energy and, very quickly, he will feel energy passing through him in the form of heat. His patient will be sitting on a low stool, allowing Andrew to move around them in whatever way he chooses. Accompanied, of course, by any spirit doctors or other helpers, who might choose to intervene.

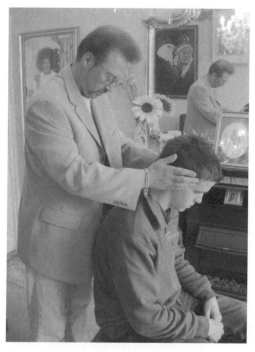

Andrew at work in his Sanctuary

Andrew will place his hands on to the patient's back, starting at the bottom of their spinal chord and working upwards to the head. By now he will be feeling the healing energies as a surge of tremendous heat coming from every part of his body. Place a thermometer in his hands, however, and it will simply register normal temperature.

Later during the session, he may also place hands directly over specific trouble spots. In any case, he will always finish the healing session by covering the eyes. It is often at this point that patients will marvel at the vivid colours they experience. Interestingly enough, their first session may present them with very dull and dingy colours – browns, blacks, greys etc. This never surprises Andrew. It merely confirms that the patient's colour imbalance is pronounced. What you see is what you've got.

Andrew at work – totally focused

Now comes the intriguing part. As the healing energy begins to work, patients may find their colours altering dramatically into the most vibrant tones – bright oranges, reds, purples, emeralds and startling blues – all playing their part in restoring energy, balance, release from pain, loss of swelling – the list is almost endless.

Pink is a particularly common colour seen during healing by tumour and cancer sufferers. For M.E. chronic fatigue syndrome sufferers it's yellow. Andrew illustrates this with two colour experiences related by patients:

The first had been diagnosed with a malignant tumour behind her eye. It was at the stage where the eyeball was protruding badly from the socket and her vision was down to ten percent of its normal capacity. The tumour was impinging badly on the optic nerve. As soon as Andrew placed his hands over her eye she saw a very bright pink colour. A week later the improvement she reported in her eyesight was incredible. She was keen to share her good luck with her specialist, instantly regretting having done so, however. His reaction was to rubbish her story.

Andrew is obviously on a short fuse when he recalls how easily such a triumph in healing can be trashed without a second thought by the medical profession.

"A medical professional practising with a closed mind is, in my opinion, a threat to society. Whereas a medical professional practising with an open mind, inspired by love, is a true asset to society."

The second colour testimony he cites concerns an M.E. sufferer. The lady in question, aged in her sixties, had suffered with the syndrome for over five years. As soon as Andrew placed his hands over her eyes, she saw bright yellows. They stayed with her for ten minutes or so and, at the end of her session, she was astounded that the 'flu-like aches she had become accustomed to were completely absent. Andrew also recalls actually seeing her entire body surrounded by a yellow glow. Her recovery was whistlestop.

Andrew keeps on repeating like well-worn mantras his profound belief that *"Colour Represents Energy"* and *"Colour and Heat Go Together"*. And, without a shadow of a doubt, he believes that the heat generated by the healing force is inexplicably intense, powerful and enduring.

He recalls taking part in a UK radio programme, hosted by one of the South Coast's popular presenters. She was pretty blunt in her obviously detached scepticism to begin with but couldn't resist asking Andrew on air to provide some healing for a neck problem. As usual, he started at the base of the spine and the heat seemed fairly modest. At this stage the presenter was looking pretty smug in her judgement of what was happening. By the time he was half way up, however, she was shrieking out loud that his hands were like an electric bar fire. So shaken was she by the experience, she had to go home. And, so impressed was she, she then attended Andrew's Healing Sanctuary in her own right.

Intense heat, jewel-like colours, total relaxation, rapid release from stiffness, pain and swelling. These, I have noted, each time we talk about Andrew's methods, are the usual, shared experiences. However, somewhat alarmingly, he then mentions that his spirit doctors "sometimes put needles in". Patients, he says, comment that they can actually feel them going in. On top of this, the sensations can accompany them home. He's had reports of patients awaking in their own beds to see a hand placing a needle into the centre of their forehead. "Ouch", I mouth …

A little bit too much information now.

Once again, I am forced to recognise that so much of what Andrew does in his spiritual healing process, simply defies logical analysis. He is trying so hard to demonstrate to me how it all functions, every day in his healing room, rain or shine. This is the reality of his life. It might not be the reality of mine.

But then who's to say that *mine* is the definitive template?

Back to the "Take-away" discussion we were having. This "mobile healing effect" also produces for some patients the most fascinating symptoms well after their treatment session at the Sanctuary. Andrew highlights the case of Keith, who required healing for a huge number of tumours on his body. He was literally crying when he approached Andrew for help, distraught and worn out with the strain of his condition.

Later that night, Keith was awoken in bed by red-hot burning all over his body. Although he was lying in a totally dark room, he saw colours all around the space. On switching on the bedroom light, he and his wife were amazed to discover that he had bright-red hand prints on his back, just where Andrew had placed his hands earlier in the day. Keith's tumours vanished.

One-off, decidedly odd things also happen from time to time, which Andrew believes are a result of the tremendous energy surge his healing can create. He remembers placing his hands on a lady suffering with M.E. at a group healing session in Brighton some ten years ago. Half way through the session she suddenly gave a shriek and began crawling around on the floor. Her ring had exploded into three pieces. The ring was analysed and there were no stress breaks in the metal. *"Don't worry"*, reassures Andrew. *"It doesn't usually happen!"*

Another time recently a patient left the healing room, got into his car parked outside and then needed urgently to make a business telephone call. But his mobile battery was completely dead when he picked up the handset. He panicked a bit because the call was very important – as he did so, he felt heat shooting down his arm and into the handset. The phone charged to full.

Andrew confirms that he is never, ever blasé about someone coming to him for treatment. He tries to be modest about his impressive hit rate and the miraculous U-turns his powers seem to bully illnesses into making. Part of his success, he believes, is down to his refusal to accept that some illnesses aren't curable. He believes very strongly in reincarnation, with each lifetime spent here an opportunity to right wrongs, learn lessons unheeded from previous incarnations and generally put one's house in order. He is convinced that the world follows a universal karmic pattern. When you're here you should try to acquire as many "Brownie points" as you possibly can. Shape up and ship out, a better person each time.

So, why do good people get ill then? I ask. We're back to the karmic pattern. For some, illness will teach them their own, individual lessons. For others, their illness will help someone else learn overdue lessons. But, no illness is incurable. On that Andrew is adamant.

And, alarmingly, Andrew is also adamant that most "spiritual healers" don't get the job done. If you're thinking of consulting one, you're probably choosing the healer at a time when you're not at your best. And you're likely to find someone unlikely to deliver the goods. So why bother. Why waste valuable and precious time.

OK Andrew, I say. Point taken. But now I'm at a loss to know just how one does ever manage to cross the path of an Andrew McKellar. How does one pinpoint a potential miracle worker? Needle and haystack are a pretty daunting proposition. The reality is that spiritual healers aren't there in Yellow Pages with the equivalent of the gas fitter's CORGI registration, are they? They don't come with "Genuine" plastered across their forehead.

Precisely why, when you do meet a healer for the first time you should hold back on expecting a healing session. Instead use your appointment to do some background research on the healer. Ask to see testimonials from satisfied patients. If this doesn't go down well? Well, you've probably got your answer. Any properly gifted spiritual healer will come with obvious credentials: grateful letters, articles from the press, even patient interviews on video sometimes. If your prospective healer balks at your questions, would you honestly want to put yourself in their hands anyway?

No, you wouldn't. When you buy a toolkit you check its contents. When you consult your colour chart it's not unreasonable to expect the shop to have pots of paint. Seeing a spiritual healer is a bit like choosing DIY over having the decorators in. You have an empty canvass on which to paint. So, why skimp on materials?

"WALLPAPER"

*"The good-hearted man, who professes to no religion,
is the truly religious man"*

Sai Baba

We are discussing Andrew's views on religion. It's a topic passionately close to his heart. Time and again he is at pains to reinforce that his work is inspired, motivated and driven only by sincere love and compassion for fellow human beings. It is nothing to do with any formal religion. He will treat anyone – absolutely anyone – in need of help.

What – even a thoroughly no good, convicted murderer? I ask. A no-hoper serial killer? Too right he will. And, in true DIY terminology, just like his "bag of tools" comparisons, we are now talking wallpaper department.

"I would definitely treat a convicted murderer. Who am I to judge? I'm just the channel for this vast power coming through. Let's face it, we all make mistakes. I've made bucketloads. My healing is unconditional. Life is like wallpapering a room. When you first start, inevitably some sheets you hang will be lopsided; they might not match up – or worse, some of them will come down. But, if we try to do better over a period of time, with practice we start to improve. The wallpaper stays up."

Andrew is defiantly non-religious. He has a horror of being "pigeon-holed" and is convinced that history and its horrendously long record of violence and prejudice, should be more than enough to teach future generations how to get it right. This thing called love thy neighbour.

"Just look back a few hundred years. There were gifted psychics and healers around, who were good, caring and loving people. What did religious people do? They drowned them; they burned them; they judged them as witches and warlocks, not recognising that mediumistically-inspired healing was around for years before religious faiths were even created."

So, has he been the target of religious prejudice? And how. One of the worst "bible-thumping" onslaughts came from a lady, branding him in a newspaper letter as the Devil himself. Jesus Christ was the only person capable of performing miracles, she raged. Christ would be returning soon, she warned, and Andrew should accept that only through Him could he reach God. Jesus died to save us from our sins …

Clearly, these two were unlikely to see eye to eye.

This was a rare occasion where Andrew felt compelled to respond. He suggested that the Devil was simply a fictitious creation of the church, used by historical religious leaders to recruit and control by fear. "Jesus dying on the cross to save us from our sins", he believes is one of Christianity's biggest cop-outs for the avoidance of self-responsibility. Perhaps when Jesus did pitch up, she would like to redirect Him to Andrew's home, he suggested. He would look forward to having tea with J.C. and they could both discuss how some Christians appear to assume the right to speak in His name. That would surely trouble Him sufficiently to need a bit of Andrew's healing.

For severe depression …

Andrew is also vehemently against being dubbed "faith" healer. His gift is open to all, he stresses. It has no boundaries. All are deserving. Belief in a God is simply irrelevant for healing energy to work. Healing is about giving unconditionally. It's way beyond faith. Religion for Andrew is just a decorative label. There are other ways he chooses to be and they stem from his commitment to helping others as actively and positively as he can:

"*Love is action. Service is action*", he often repeats and, I confess, as one listens it certainly does begin to rub off and make eminent sense.

And then we get on to how a spiritual healer's gift is usually defined by mainstream medical experts. By now Andrew's patience is obviously wearing a bit thin.

> *"The medical profession usually refers to spiritual healing as 'complementary' therapy"*, he sighs. *"What they should be saying is 'alternative' therapy. It's way, way different."*

Perhaps he's just getting tired of papering over their cracks.

"KNOTS"

Man is tied in many knots.

He is like a piece of rope stretching to breaking point.

If he opens to divine love …

The knots will soften and finally disperse.

The rope will slacken and become more flexible.

All tension and stress shall ease and finally disappear.

Then, gradually, the rope shall turn into a golden thread.

**Received in a meditative state
By Andrew McKellar**

CHAPTER TEN

CHAPTER TEN

SEPARATE PATHS, MOVING WORDS

"For every event that occurs, there will follow another event,
whose existence was caused by the first.
And this second event will be pleasant or unpleasant,
according to its cause"

The above is a law of karma, as taught by the Buddhist faith. And, during the time spent meeting with Andrew McKellar to discuss his biography, I have learnt that his wife Gerri, in addition to being a developing psychic medium in her own right, is also a keen and committed student of Buddhism. Andrew and Gerri have always given me the impression that their relationship was "meant to be". They have so much in common in their spiritual interests.

So it comes as a huge bombshell to learn suddenly from Andrew that he and Gerri are separating. Gerri has moved from Burridge with the children to another nearby village and their half-moon drive house, so vividly predicted in Gerri's dream a couple of years ago, suddenly has a "For Sale" sign out front.

Time to move on

"*We both agree that we were brought together spiritually to help one another to progress*", Andrew says.

"*Gerri is a gentle type. She wants peace and quiet to devote herself to her personal, spiritual development. She needs a harmonious atmosphere. The past couple of years have been very pressurised. I've lost both my parents, we've had to deal with the local council reviewing the number of patients I can treat each week and then there is the sheer weight of visitors to the Sanctuary – not just the patients but also the interest from the press and television.*"

I ask Andrew how he feels about it all. This is surely major stuff. Is he OK with it?

"*Actually, I was devastated at first. Floored. But then I realised that I'm quite a rough and rugged type – the opposite of Gerri, if you like. I can cope with waves being made. It's inevitable with the gift I've been given that my name will become more famous. People need healing. People are curious. I can cope with it. Gerri would prefer not to. I respect that.*"

Well, did Andrew have any inkling of these sudden changes? I ask.

"*It's funny you should ask,*" replies Andrew. "*Recently I had a very profound dream and it puzzled me. I dreamt that Gerri was ill and needed healing. She was coming to the Sanctuary for treatment sessions. But she was living somewhere else. I told her about it at the time. Neither of us realised how prophetic it was.*"

Andrew refuses to view his marriage separation in any negative light. This present chapter in his life doesn't have to be viewed as the "unpleasant" side of karma. This is no setback. For Andrew McKellar it is an opportunity to move forward. Just as it is for Gerri too. And he is determined to make what lies ahead a pleasant experience. He is actually glad, he admits, that his house is on the market. Living in Burridge has taught him a considerable amount about human nature – most of it leaving him with a nasty taste in the mouth. Even though he was able to gain permission from the local council to run his Sanctuary from home, he has been painfully aware that numbers of patients have been woefully restricted. Each week sees him juggling the ever-present list of potential patients – some absolutely desperate to be seen. He feels very positive about finding new premises and is now sure that he won't make the same mistakes he made when he chose his present location:

"The right place will come up. I just know it's out there. My patients will follow me anywhere. I know some are worried that I'll move to America. The truth is I believe I will travel between the UK and the USA each year. There's no way I would abandon them. I stick by people – always."

Andrew clearly trusts his spiritual guides implicitly and without reservation. He requires no proof that his present difficulties will metamorphose into positive results. He seems to accept that change is a natural progression and is positively energised to move on, create a new home for the Sanctuary and push down any boundaries he may encounter en route. I am reminded of a saying, which surely could never be more apt than for Andrew at this crucial and somehow poignant time:

"Change is inevitable. Growth is intentional."

"I'm going to kick down the doors of scepticism. I'm going to make tidal waves for spiritual healing. I have total confidence in my ability to produce mass results. If I have to hire the Albert Hall to expand spiritual healing out into the world, then I will. Whatever it takes. I shall cure thousands of people as a channel. Nothing will stand in my way."

Without wishing to sound presumptuous, I ask Andrew just how he's going to afford, financially, to follow this path. After all, I point out, his fee for healing services is modest by anyone's standards. In fact, as modest goes, it's minuscule.

"Yes", he says, *"of course you have to earn enough money to fund the right premises to run a sanctuary. You do need accommodation and the wherewithal to make ends meet. But money comes to those who need it. As each day unfolds, so do amazing possibilities. It's a progressional thing and it doesn't mean ever having to abandon the ordinary Joe Bloggs."*

"*I know only too well what it's like to be at rock bottom. I can't pass someone homeless and on the streets without stopping to talk with them and give them money. I speak to tramps and bag ladies. The memory of being alone and penniless never leaves you. Even today I live in a beautiful house but I still stare at a tin of beans in the supermarket and think what a pleasure it is to be able to buy it. I don't take anything for granted. And I never will.*"

And, you know what? I believe him.

Andrew McKellar has come a long way in his forty years. His was not the most fortunate of childhoods. His was not the easiest lot in life. Many a person in his shoes would have sunk permanently in a sea of 'poor me' and short straws. They would have earned themselves a reputation for perpetually moaning 'Why me?' and doing their utmost to drag others well and truly down to their level of all alone misery.

Instead, Andrew McKellar has chosen to view himself not as victim but as victor. He is one of the chosen few. One of a select, rarely met fragment of society, dedicating endless time to helping others. Bringing hope and a newfound purpose to countless people for whom time has become frighteningly finite from the instant their illness became fact.

Andrew McKellar has learned that his is a privileged life – a voyage of discovery guided from above. A gift.

"*The journey continues*", he beams. "*I can't wait. Give it a couple more years and we'll be starting the next book. It's going to be absolutely wonderful.*"

And, you know what? I still believe him.

Because the book is already in the pen.

"We make a living by what we get.
We make a life by what we give"

LONG LIFE ALKALINE

"Light of Love"

Why do you not know God?
Why do you not feel God?

You have been given the torch
of true happiness and bliss

But you must supply the batteries –
The batteries of Love

Andrew McKellar

Acknowledgements

There is always the niggling worry that people will be left out in the "grateful thanks" bit. However, most of the people I know wouldn't care a fig because they already appreciate how much they are valued. Such is the bonus of having "spiritually-inclined" friends.

Firstly, enormous thanks to the various "anonymous" individuals, whose food-for-thought quotations have been included in each chapter in the biography. Wherever a quotation, poem, piece of prose or image has been featured, the relevant person has been credited.

Secondly, I must thank Andrew McKellar for all our evening get-togethers, come ice, rain or shine. Finding photographs and creative pieces to include in the book at a time when one's house is packed up to move, one's neighbours are not big on healing, one's patients are lining up for treatment, one's marriage is under review and one's people-friendly animals need feeding, cannot have been easy. But he made it so.

Which brings me to everyone else.

Tremendous thanks to Andrew's patients featured throughout the book – Malcolm, Veronica, Les, Dianne, Harry, Cath, Robin, Eileen, David, Edna, Ivor, Pat, Sue, Terri, Trevor, Ian and his Mum, Betty, Freda, Audrey, June, Nolene, Tessa, Cathy, Lyn, Peter, Sue2, Gary, Diane, Giselle, Heather, Sharon, Sheila, Michelle and, of course, retrospectively, Anne. Their testimonies are truly heart-warming to read and never fail to cheer one up on those days when even a bar of chocolate fails to do the trick. We would have been delighted to include everyone's photographs but it would have been a practical assault course. So, sincere thanks for your words. They really do make a difference.

Grateful thanks to Oliver Gray for his advice on how to tackle the book and for originally steering us in the direction of Sarsen Press. Also, to Interact Designs' Richard Blair for designing and setting up Andrew's excellent website without so much as a grumble when any gremlins cropped up. And thanks too to Dave Small for his very savvy photographic work.

Karen Harvey must read her name here, so that I can thank her for listening to chapters in Cheltenham as they were being written and never once doubting that the book was in the roller ball.

Huge thanks to wonderfully talented psychic medium and healer Stephen Smith for introducing me to healing maestro Andrew in the first place back in 2001. Presumably he had a suspicion as to what lay ahead …

Belated thanks too to psychometric medium (and I suspect sadly 'late') Mrs Smith way back in 1972, somewhere I can't remember on the South Coast. It was the forty-five minutes spent with her quite by chance "accompanying a friend" one Sunday that profoundly altered my way of thinking about death.

I would like to send a big hug to my brother Graham Preskett for welcoming Gethyn into his music studio to compose Andrew's CD and video soundtrack which, together with this book form the "portfolio" of Andrew's website vision for 2003. Graham may not "buy into" what the biography highlights but he certainly subscribes to the "We make a life by what we give" closing sentence. Good on you, Gray.

Lastly, all my love to Gethyn, one of the world's greatest sceptics just five short years ago. Thank you for listening and for being prepared to consider that we don't know everything. I couldn't have asked for more.

Magic.

Ros Jones

About the author

Ros Jones lives on the South Coast of England with her husband Gethyn. Having originally "dated" at school in the 1970s, they were parted for over twenty years until reuniting and marrying in 1998 – proving that miracles indeed sometimes do happen!

A graduate in European languages, Ros spent many of her working years as a recruitment consultant in London, introduced to the industry in the 1970s by her sister Hazel, without whom this book would not have materialised. Until 2003, Ros's experience of writing was limited to one shaky French thesis on wonderfully outrageous author Sidonie Gabrielle Colette, several years of creating advertising copy to a deadline, hassling staff for corporate newsletters and the occasional press release.

The book is a work of love in memory of her sister Hazel – "Dink" to her family and close friends. It is also a tribute to its subject Andy McKellar – a man who does what he says, no matter how impossible the odds. Consistently.

Ros's personal dedication for the book is for Hazel – simply the nicest sister anyone, anywhere could ever have. And for her stepsons, Pascal and Bryn – a joy to know.

In loving memory of Hazel Jones
(Née Preskett)
1950-2002

"Love you lots"

ANDREW'S

"PORTFOLIO"

*"If you want to know what your true beliefs are,
take a look at your actions"*

ABSENT HEALING

From 2003 Andrew will be introducing a powerful dimension to his work via his website:

Absent Healing

By visiting his website – www.andrewmckellar.com – anyone in need of healing assistance will be able to contact him by e-mail.

The site is very easy to navigate – simply click on the **ABSENT HEALING** button and you will be taken straight to the relevant page.

It is Andrew's sincere wish to reach as many people as possible throughout the world. He appreciates the sense of urgency people often experience when they discover they have an illness, or when they are suddenly aware that a loved one is suffering. The need to do "something" is overwhelming.

Distance in the field of spiritual healing is irrelevant.

All are welcome. Always.

*"One meets one's destiny often in
the road one takes to avoid it"*

French Proverb